SHAKE-SPEARE

The Mystery

BY

GEORGE ELLIOTT SWEET

to
Salem College Library

Compliments of the author

This book is copy number ...5̄3̄0̄...
of the limited first edition

George Elliott Sweet

822.33
A2S

© 1956 BY GEORGE ELLIOTT SWEET

PRINTED IN THE UNITED STATES OF AMERICA
BY STANFORD UNIVERSITY PRESS

First edition, May 1956

Library of Congress Catalog Card Number: 56-9651

To my son, JERRY

Foreword

By Erle Stanley Gardner

Detective work has always fascinated me.

We are accustomed to think of detective work only in connection with crime, but some of the most fascinating detective work of all time has been in fields other than those having to do with crime.

The astronomer is one of the greatest of all detectives. Standing on a speck of cosmic dust, his mind encased in a body which can reach only a few brief inches, the astronomer has, nevertheless, projected his mind into the endless infinity of space so that he can tell with certainty the mass of some huge sun so far away that it takes light from that sun hundreds of thousands of years to reach us. The astronomer can tell whether such a sun is approaching us or whether it is receding, and approximate its velocity. He can tell many of the chemical constituents of such a sun as well as determine its size and mass.

The physicist, dealing with particles of matter so small that they baffle the most powerful microscopes, can not only prove the existence of particles the human eye can never hope to see, but can demonstrate the laws which govern the arrangements of such particles, can alter the arrangement and release forces so infinitely destructive they threaten a cosmic cataclysm.

Recently we have heard about the "literary detective." Here again we have one of the most fascinating applications of detective work conceivable. Long after an era has vanished into the realm of history, the literary detective, using his powers of reasoning, can penetrate secrets which were so well kept the persons who lived in that era had no inkling of them.

A few weeks ago, Elliott Sweet came to my ranch with my friend Bill Pemberton. Sweet started talking to me about Shakespeare and I suddenly realized that I was in the presence of one of the outstanding literary detectives of the day.

Sweet's theories fascinated me. I studied his manuscript, I

I

talked with him, and the more I thought about the problem he presented the more fascinated I became.

One would need to be an expert on Shakespeare, as I am not, to attempt to argue the technical points involved in Elliott Sweet's book. I will, however, enthusiastically attest to the persuasive logic and to the enchanting development of the historic mystery plot in this manuscript.

Sweet's findings are supported by an interesting body of proof. There is, moreover, something so completely logical about the manner in which his mind moves from point to point, that one realizes his presentation is indicative of remarkable skill in collecting the facts, presenting them and thereafter drawing a logical conclusion from them. I think perhaps the best test of all, however, is that having once read this manuscript I simply can't forget it. I find myself thinking of it a dozen times a week.

Regardless of how logical a theory may be, regardless of how smoothly it may be presented, it is very, very difficult to present any idea to the human mind in this day of rapid-fire existence which can create a truly lasting impression.

The hectic nature of our lives, the speed with which developments take place, the threatening forces of destruction which are now poised ready to be unleashed, keep our minds so busily engaged in making social, economic, and civic adjustment that it is difficult to retain impressions. We are like chips which have been floating placidly along a smooth current to the outer brim of a whirlpool. We are swinging around in a circle which is constantly moving faster and faster until we feel ourselves at the very vortex of a psychic whirlpool into which our lives have been plunged.

It takes writing of a high order, and thinking of the most persuasive sort, to crash through that tempo and create a lasting impression in the mind.

When you read Sweet's comments on Shakespeare, I think you will find that he has accomplished this all but impossible task. You may be able to put the book down, but I doubt if you will ever be able to forget the point he has made in that book.

To my mind, that is the mark of a great writer and a great literary detective.

ERLE STANLEY GARDNER
March 1956

Table of Contents

3

Chapter I

THE PROBLEM

> "Not mine own fears, nor the prophetic soul
> Of the wide world dreaming on things to come,
> Can yet the lease of my true love control,
> Suppos'd as forfeit to a confin'd doom.
> The mortal moon hath her eclipse endur'd,
> And the sad augurs mock their own presage;
> Incertainties now crown themselves assur'd,
> And peace proclaims olives of endless age.
> Now with the drops of this most balmy time
> My love looks fresh, and Death to me subscribes,
> Since, spite of him, I'll live in this poor rime,
> While he insults o'er dull and speechless tribes:
> And thou in this shalt find thy monument,
> When tyrants' crests and tombs of brass are spent."

Shake-speare—*Sonnet 107*

The literary world has been in disagreement as to the identity of Shake-speare since 1769, nearly two centuries. If new light is to be thrown upon this old problem in the present age, the so-called Scientific Age, the logical approach would seem to be a scientific approach. Science might best be served by dethroning all of the candidates (William Shakspere, Francis Bacon, Sir Walter Raleigh, Mary, Countess of Pembroke, the Earls of Oxford, Rutland, and Derby, and Sir Edward Dyer) for the time being and let the Shake-speare plays, poems, and sonnets tell us what they will without any preconceived ideas (and let the dates fall where they may). This is somewhat analogous to the way in which the scientist studies the properties of a substance by controlling certain factors while allowing other factors to vary. The chemist in his hunt for the identity of an unknown compound would apply the methodical tests of qualitative analysis; the last thing he would do would be to add a second unknown to aid him in discovering the identity of

5

the first unknown. Therefore, let us think of Shake-speare merely as Shake-speare, the Great Unknown, not with the first name of William, Francis, Walter, or Mary. The First Sonnet Folio of 1609 announces "Shake-speare" as its author (no first name given). Roughly half of the Quartos of the plays use the hyphenated form for Shake-speare and we shall adopt this spelling of the writer's name.

The statisticians tell us that the vocabulary of the average university graduate is about three to four thousand words; of some of the most eminent men in literary history less than ten thousand words; Shake-speare employed approximately fifteen thousand different words in composing his works. Such a vocabulary, never equaled or even approached by any other writer, could only be acquired by constant and consistent reading from early youth to old age. Shake-speare must have loved books; he must have had a fine library, perhaps the finest library of his time. Shake-speare borrowed freely from other authors. Of the thirty-seven Shake-speare plays all have plots from known sources save three, *Love's Labour's Lost*, *The Tempest*, and *A Midsummer Night's Dream*. To have known where to go for his thirty-four borrowed plots Shake-speare must have read practically everything published in English, French, Italian, Greek, and Latin. But he was in no sense of the word a bookworm—he was a man of the world. He knew thousands of people intimately. He talked with and studied every class and condition of mankind and every class and condition of womankind. Sir Walter Scott put it very well when he said of Shake-speare, "It is difficult to compare him to any other individual. The only one to whom I can compare him is that wonderful Arabian dervish who dived into the body of each [person] and in that way became familiar with the thoughts and secrets of their hearts." Samuel Coleridge called Shake-speare "myriad-minded." Shake-speare loved people—or at least people had a vital and vivid fascination for him. He enjoyed writing; he felt a compulsion to express his thoughts in writing, and we imagine that, in all probability, he was still writing the year he died.

Writers on Shake-speare sometimes adopt diametrically opposite viewpoints. Thus George Bernard Shaw disagrees with Frank Harris: "Frank conceived Shakespear to have been a broken-hearted, melancholy, enormously sentimental person, whereas

I am convinced that he was very like myself; . . ." We must go along with Shaw; both Shaw and Shake-speare were pragmatic extroverts. Both expressed their ideas in down-to-earth realistic writing. Neither man was a "light cougher"; they both let the world know in no uncertain terms that they expected their literary efforts to live through the ages.

In the preface to his play the *Dark Lady of the Sonnets,* Shaw makes some pertinent observations about Shake-speare:

> "I suggest that Shakespear missed this questionable advantage, not because he was socially too low to have attained it, but because he conceived himself as belonging to the upper class from which our public school boys are now drawn.
>
> "He was not stupid either: if his class limitation and a profession that cut him off from actual participation in great affairs of State had not confined his opportunities of intellectual and political training to private conversation and to the Mermaid Tavern, he probably would have become one of the ablest men of his time instead of being merely its ablest playwright.
>
> "I lay stress on this irony of Shakespear's, this impish rejoicing in pessimism, this exultation in what breaks the hearts of common men, not only because it is diagnostic of that immense energy of life which we call genius . . .
>
> "In view of these facts, it is dangerous to cite Shakespear's pessimism as evidence of the despair of a heart broken by the Dark Lady. There is an irrepressible gaiety of genius which enables it to bear the whole weight of the world's misery without blenching. There is a laugh ready to avenge its tears of discouragement.
>
> "Is it not clear that to the last there was in Shakespear an incorrigible divine levity, an inexhaustible joy that derided sorrow? Think of the poor Dark Lady having to stand up to this unbearable power of extracting a grim fun from everything. Mr. Harris writes as if Shakespear did all the suffering and the Dark Lady all the cruelty. But

why does he not put himself in the Dark Lady's place for a moment as he has put himself so successfully in Shakespear's? Imagine her reading the hundred and thirtieth sonnet.

"Now whoever will read *Lear* and *Measure for Measure* will find stamped on his mind such an appalled sense of the danger of dressing man in a little brief authority, such a merciless stripping of the purple from the 'poor, bare, forked animal' that calls itself a king and fancies itself a god, that one wonders what was the real nature of the mysterious restraint that kept 'Eliza and our James' from teaching Shakespear to be civil to crowned heads . . .

"If such evidence can prove anything Shakespear loathed courtiers.

"Then consider Shakespear's kings and lords and gentlemen! Surely a more mercilessly exposed string of scoundrels never crossed the stage.

"His first and last word on parliament was, 'Get thee glass eyes, and, like a scurvy politician, seem to see the thing thou dost not!' "

If we are to classify Shake-speare in his own age we must call him one of the University Wits—which is not to say he was necessarily a graduate of either Cambridge or Oxford; he might have taken some other route, as Thomas Kyd did, to gain his intimate knowledge of the classics. In one sense Shake-speare was all of the University Wits combined, for he copied the writing methods of each and every one of them and was enormously indebted to John Lyly, Thomas Kyd, George Peele, Christopher Marlowe, and Robert Greene. Sidney Lee says, "Superior as Shakespeare's powers were to those of Marlowe, his coadjustor in *Henry VI*, the early tragedies often reveal him in the character of a faithful disciple of that vehement delineator of tragic passion. Shakespeare's early comedies disclose a like relationship between him and Lyly." Lee continues, "There is internal proof that Marlowe worked on earlier plays of Shakespeare. . . . All the blank verse

in Shakespeare's early plays bears the stamp of Marlowe's inspiration."

Charles Lamb writes, "The reluctant pangs of abdicating
royalty in *Edward II* furnished hints which Shakespeare scarcely
improved in his *Richard II*." G. B. Harrison expresses Shake-
speare's debenture thus, "A comparison between Marlowe's *Jew
of Malta* and *Edward II* and Shakespeare's *Merchant of Venice*
and *Richard II* will show how much he was indebted to Marlowe."
Harrison also notes the similarity to Lyly's manner of composition:
"The comedy of *Love's Labour's Lost*, written in a euphuistic
strain, is probably his first complete play."

Since Shake-speare imitated all of the University Wits, the
logical conclusion is that he was a *complete contemporary* of the
University Wits. There is a definite possibility that he was inspired
to write by John Lyly at the height of Lyly's fame. John Lyly's
novels, *Euphues* and *Euphues and His England,* published about
1579 and 1580, made him the outstanding figure in English literature and the darling of the court. Shake-speare mimicked the
style and mannerisms of Lyly in his early comedies. Ivor Brown
says:

> "Lyly wrote comedies whose lyrics are far better than
> their dialogue, which was streaked with elaborate conceits.
> Every young writer with a quick, ingenious hand enjoys
> playing with words, and Shakespeare never wholly tired
> of this juggling, for which he had an infinite aptitude.
> The earliest plays are full of puns and Lylyan patterning
> of words."

Lyly's fame was on the decline before 1590; Greene and
especially Marlowe held the center of the stage in the late eighties
and early nineties. Shake-speare was much too agile of foot and
pen to follow the Lylyan methods into their descendancy. Shake-
speare's adaptation of Marlowe's "mighty line" to his own uses
must have been soon after the appearance of *Tamburlaine, the
Great* (about 1586–87), Marlowe's first striking success. The two
Shake-speare plays that the majority of the critics contend were
by dual authorship were *2 Henry VI* and *3 Henry VI*, which
they say was a collaboration by Marlowe and Shake-speare. Now,
Henry VI is not mature Marlowe; it is youthful Marlowe and

must be placed as roughly contemporary with *Tamburlaine*. Edmund Malone, one of the most careful and exacting of Shake-speare devotees, thought *Henry VI* was written about 1586, but he did not acknowledge Shake-speare as its co-writer. Malone believed that either Marlowe and Greene or Marlowe alone wrote *King Henry VI*. While we shall adopt the opinion of the majority of critics that Shake-speare and Marlowe were collaborators of *Henry VI*, we feel that Malone must have been approximately correct as to the date of composition. From the immaturities of history-play style in *Henry VI* we conclude that this was one of the earliest efforts of Shake-speare in the field of the chronicle or history play. Here, then, is our first date clue. What was Christopher Marlowe doing in 1586–87 that would link him to some one of the various contenders for the Shake-speare crown?

There is abundant evidence that Shake-speare came first under the influence of Lyly, Kyd, and Peele; second, under the domination of Marlowe's "mighty line," and lastly appropriated the techniques of Greene and to a lesser degree the style of Thomas Nashe and Thomas Lodge. Lyly's blank verse play *The Woman in the Moon* he terms his first work, which would place it in the late seventies with his two novels. Most of Lyly's comedy dramas had been written by the mid-eighties. The composition date of Thomas Kyd's epic *The Spanish Tragedy* can be placed no more accurately than merely somewhere between 1579 and 1586. Shake-speare's *Titus Adronicus* plainly used *The Spanish Tragedy* as a model. In both these productions blood flowed in rivers over the stage in true melodramatic fashion. Shake-speare went on to produce great tragedy; so far as we know, Thomas Kyd remained true to the revenge ideals of Seneca. We would know more about the mature Kyd and more about Shake-speare's indebtedness to him if the whole of Kyd's *Hamlet* were not lost. George Peele gave to Shake-speare much of his ear for the musical sound of words, yet the Shake-speare lyrics and the Shake-speare mastery of word-music exceeded those fine qualities in Peele. We cannot censor Shake-speare too severely for his appropriation of the writings and style of the other University Wits, because he bested each and every one of them at their own game. Without the help of these seven contemporaries, Shake-speare never would have written his mature plays, but we must remember that mature

Shake-speare was superior to mature Lyly, mature Kyd, and even mature Marlowe. Shake-speare was at least Greene's equal in wit and character portrayal.

Is it conceivable that all of Shake-speare's plays might have been written by the collaboration of Marlowe and Greene? Marlowe and Greene certainly had the capacity of the best of Shake-speare's works. Marlowe had two inferior abilities: his heroines lacked subtle grace, and he was deficient in his sense of humor. Robert Greene was able to fill in both of these defects in Marlowe; the beautiful word-portraits of mature womanhood of Greene were every bit as charming as Shake-speare's mature heroines. Marlowe in collaboration with Greene might well explain the genius of Shake-speare except for the pair's untimely deaths— Robert Greene in 1592 and Christopher Marlowe in 1593. The Greene-Marlowe genius was bright enough to be Shake-speare. They simply did not live long enough to be Shake-speare.

Shake-speare possessed the fine art of extracting from his various teachers only the best portions of their manner and style. Herein lies the true genius of the man, his arduous labors, and infinite patience in perfecting and maturing the best dramatic efforts of his contemporary University Wits. John Keats explains:

> ". . . several things dovetailed in my mind, and at once struck me what quality went to form a man of achievement, especially in literature, and which Shakespear possessed so enormously — I mean NEGATIVE CAPABILITY, that is when a man is capable of being in uncertainties, mysteries, doubts, without any irritable reaching after fact and reason."

Negative Capability has many facets. Negative Capability is the striving to perfect the imperfect. Negative Capability is involved in the willingness to aim for the betterment of an existing plot rather than to attempt a new and novel situation. Shake-speare had the happy faculty of holding his own literary style in suspension while mixing into it the best of the ingredients from the styles of his fellows. The wholesome appreciation of the capacities of your contemporary writers is a high form of literary astuteness. The ability to blend the best of several literary styles into a masterful new literary technique is a rare achievement.

Marlowe no doubt possessed more native dramatic ability than Shake-speare. *Tamburlaine, the Great* burst on the stage like a bombshell, so new and powerful was this "mighty line." Shake-speare was less spectacular but in the long run more successful. Whom did Shake-speare seek as collaborator to formulate an appropriate history-play design? The best dramatic brain of that era was procured to be Shake-speare's co-worker. Here again is Negative Capability. Shake-speare was improving and perfecting, changing and harmonizing through a long and painstaking apprenticeship. He did not reach maturity overnight; at least a decade of experimentation, recasting, and rewriting was necessary to put together Shake-speare's mighty line. All this is Negative Capability. You may rest assured that when you spot the Elizabethan with the greatest Negative Capability, you will have discovered Shake-speare.

Chapter II

THE QUEST BEGINS

"I remember it well.
'Tis since the earthquake now eleven years; . . ."

Romeo and Juliet

On a November evening in 1954 I sat and stared at the above two lines. A revelation thrust itself into my eyes; an idea so startling as to leave the mind gasping for oxygen, and yet the idea was as simple as sunshine. *Romeo and Juliet* was Shake-speare's first mature tragedy. SOMETIME DURING THE COMPOSITION OF *Romeo and Juliet* SHAKE-SPEARE MUST HAVE REALIZED THAT THIS PLAY MADE HIM THE BEST LIVING PLAYWRIGHT. *Romeo and Juliet* was the treasured landmark in Shake-speare's career, and it is here we would expect him to establish a date for his dramatic triumph and to establish the number of years occupied in his rise to this dramatic triumph. With earlier plays he had surpassed Lyly, Kyd, and Peele. Now he had topped Christopher Marlowe, for Marlowe had written no tragedies as commendable as *Romeo and Juliet*. With the subtle delineation of the character of Juliet, Shake-speare had equaled the "Homer of Women," Robert Greene, in the art of feminine character portrayal (Shake-speare was superior to Greene in general writing skill).

The memorable London earthquake occurred in 1580, which would place the Shake-speare labors on *Romeo and Juliet* in the year 1591. *Romeo and Juliet* is the only Shake-speare play which dates itself in the main body of the play. For a discussion of the controversial dating of *King Henry V* in the prologue to the fifth act of that play, see Appendix C. Shake-speare used the earthquake device to record for posterity his arrival at the top of the dramatic ladder and to establish the approximate year he started his climb upward (1580). The point has already been made that John Lyly was at the peak of his considerable fame about 1579–80; Lyly was Shake-speare's first contemporary drama teacher; Shake-speare would likely start in Lyly's steps at the height of the literary applause for John Lyly.

Now, if Shake-speare saw fit to leave a date clue when he reached dramatic maturity, he might also be expected to leave a date clue or date clues when he had accomplished the same maturity in his poetry. Shake-speare's only mature poetry was his sonnets. My next undertaking was to check for date clues in the sonnets.

The 1609 First Sonnet Folio contains a total of 154 sonnets, which may be divided into three groups: the main body of the sonnets (1 to 126 inclusive), largely concerned with "my lovely boy"; 26 sonnets (127 to 152 inclusive), mostly addressed to the "dark lady," and 2 sonnets (153 and 154), dealing with Cupid's powers. To the three major mysteries of the sonnets (the identity of the lovely boy, the identity of the dark lady, and the identity of the rival poet) can be added a whole flock of minor mysteries. These hidden secrets are much too involved to discuss at this time and must wait until we arrive at the chapter on the sonnets, when the additional three mysteries in the dedication of the sonnets (who is Mr. W. H.?; the identity of the "onlie begetter"; and, what is meant by "our ever-living poet"?) will also come up for discussion and dissection.

Right now the only relevant subject is the development of the time-scale. When were the sonnets written? The best-known "time sonnet" is 107, which is reproduced at the beginning of chapter I. In the nineteenth century, Samuel Butler interpreted the *"mortal moon"* as the defeat of the Spanish Armada and gave the composition date of Sonnet 107 as about August 8, 1588. Butler used Sonnet 104, which we might term the "elapsed time sonnet," to arrive at April 1585 for the time of the writing of Sonnet 1. He also concluded that most of the "dark lady" sonnets were composed in the fall of 1585. Butler assigned dates to all of the sonnets except four of the "dark lady" sonnets and the two "Cupid" sonnets. His composition dates ranged from April 1585 to December 1588.

Leslie Hotson, writing on the sonnets in 1949, also thought Sonnet 107 referred to the defeat of the Armada. He discovered two more "time sonnets"—Sonnet 123 and Sonnet 124. Hotson placed the composition of all three "time sonnets" in the year 1589.

He used Sonnet 104 to arrive at the conclusion that the main body of the sonnets had been written from 1586 to 1589.

Petruccio Ubaldino in *A Discourse Concerninge The Spanish Fleete, 1588* says, "Their fleete was placed in battell araie, after the manner of a Moone cressant, . . ." The horns of the fleet (moon) were turned toward the shore to form a net so that no English ships might slip through. Sir Francis Drake and his hearty sea dogs had no thought of escape. With a few small vessels the English outmaneuvered and outfought the Spaniards, completely routed the mighty Armada and put the "Moone cressant" into an eclipse. Now that Butler and Hotson have shown the way, the meaning of the four lines of Sonnet 107 becomes intelligible:

> "The mortal moon hath her eclipse endur'd
> And the sad augurs mock their own presage;
> Incertainties now crown themselves assur'd,
> And peace proclaims olives of endless age."

Mr. Hotson shows that the second line of Sonnet 123, "Thy pyramids built up with newer might," refers to the work of Pope Sixtus V in restoring four Egyptian obelisks in the years 1586, 1587, 1588, and 1589. The Pope died in the year 1590.

Sonnet 123

> "No, Time, thou shalt not boast that I do change:
> *Thy pyramids built up with newer might*
> To me are nothing novel, nothing strange;
> They are but dressings of a former sight.
> Our dates are brief, and therefore we admire
> What thou dost foist upon us that is old;
> And rather make them born to our desire
> Than think that we before have heard them told.
> Thy registers and thee I both defy,
> Not wondering at the present nor the past,
> For thy records and what we see doth lie,
> Made more or less by thy continual haste.
> This I do vow, and this shall ever be.
> I will be true, despite thy scythe and thee."

In Sonnet 124, "Fortune's bastard . . . subject to . . . Time's hate," is King Henry III of France. Late in 1588, knowing that the Duke of Guise is planning to murder him, the King simply beats Guise to the stab and, for good measure, also has Guise's brother, the Cardinal of Lorraine, killed. In August of 1589 a Dominican friar named Jacques Clement gave King Henry a message to read, but before Henry could read it the monk succeeded in avenging the brothers Guise; Clement plucked a dagger from his sleeve and stuck the French King in the belly. This is the significance of ". . . falls under the blow of thralled discontent, . . ."

Sonnet 124

"If my dear love were but the child of state
It might for *Fortune's bastard* be unfather'd
As *subject to* Time's love or to *Time's hate*,
Weeds among weeds, or flowers with flowers gather'd.
No, it was builded far from accident;
It suffers not in smiling pomp, *nor falls
Under the blow of thralled discontent*,
Whereto the inviting time our fashion calls:
It fears not policy, that heretic,
Which works on leases of short number'd hours,
But all alone stands hugely politic,
That it nor grows with heat nor drowns with showers.
To this I witness call the fools of time,
Which die for goodness, who have liv'd for crime."

On the basis of Leslie Hotson's conclusive evidence that Sonnets 107, 123 and 124 were written in the year 1589, we will adopt the premise that the main body of the sonnets was completed in 1589. The date for the writing of Sonnet 1 may be April 1586 or April 1587, depending upon the season of the year in which Sonnet 104 came into being:

Sonnet 104

"To me, fair friend, you never can be old,
For as you were when first your eye I eyed,
Such seems your beauty still. *Three winters cold
Have from the forests shook three summers' pride*,

Three beauteous springs to yellow autumn turn'd
In process of the seasons have I seen,
Three April perfumes in three hot Junes burn'd,
Since first I saw you fresh, which yet are green.
Ah! yet doth beauty, like a dial-hand,
Steal from his figure, and no pace perceiv'd;
So your sweet hue, which methinks still doth stand,
Hath motion, and mine eye may be deceiv'd:
For fear of which, hear this, thou age unbred:
Ere you were born was beauty's summer dead."

The time condition stated first in Sonnet 104 is, "Three winters cold have from the forests shook three summers' pride." The second and third time conditions, "Three beauteous springs to yellow autumn turn'd in process of the seasons have I seen, three April perfumes in three hot Junes burn'd," must of necessity conform to the first condition. If Sonnet 104 had been written in the fall the first condition would have been, "Two winters cold have from the forests shook three summers' pride." If Sonnet 104 had been written in the summer, there would have been but two winters cold and two yellow autumns to go with the three summers. If Sonnet 104 had been written in the spring, in order for there to have been three winters cold and three yellow autumns the third time condition would have to read "four April perfumes in three hot Junes burn'd." Had the season of composition been any season except winter the rhythm of three would have been upset. When cold weather had set in for the third time since the April meeting, "when first your eye I eyed," all of the time conditions for Sonnet 104 had been fulfilled. Therefore we would expect Sonnet 104 to have been written in the winter of 1589; which would make the April of Sonnet 1, April 1587. Please remember the date April 1587; this date has historical significance.

Before the completion of this chapter I shall have touched on a phase of the mystic evidence in Shake-speare. I do not term this mystic evidence excellent evidence or even good evidence, but it is certainly evidence that cannot be ignored. Inasmuch as the sixteenth century believed in the mystical sciences to a much greater extent than the twentieth century, this mystic evidence must be given serious consideration.

The fact that Shake-speare was a mature poet in April 1587, and the fact that he had no peer in dramatic writing in 1591, is of the utmost importance in establishing his identity. It is gratifying to know that the evidence for these dates is excellent evidence. This evidence is garnered from the careful analysis of all of the time-evidence in the sonnets plus the only time-evidence within the main body of a play which points out a particular year. The April 1587 date for maturity as a poet and the 1591 date for reaching dramatic pre-eminence will eliminate most of the candidates for Shake-speare honors. Shake-speare could scarcely have been another University Wit. Shake-speare surpassed all of his fellow University Wits in 1591 with the possible exception of Robert Greene, who died in 1592 and would not have had time to write the other mature Shake-speare plays. Marlowe is eliminated by the fact that his best play, *Edward II*, written in 1592 or 1593, had a puppet heroine. The creator of the divine Juliet in 1591 would not have produced a wooden Isabella in 1592 or 1593. It is doubtful if any English writers except Greene and Shake-speare have been able to paint womanhood in the lifelike, flesh-and-blood manner in which Juliet is painted. Shake-speare's "mighty huntresses" have bared the female soul to public view.

With the advent of *Romeo and Juliet*, Shake-speare had sharpened all of his tools of keen and witty dialogue and was ready to write not only mature tragedy but mature chronicle and mature comedy as well. Since Shake-speare had reached mature stature as a dramatist by 1591, the corollary assumption is that all or nearly all of his workshop plays, his experimental plays, his immature plays lay behind him. There would appear to be at least one exception. *The Merry Wives of Windsor* evidently came after 1591, but it was hasty work and might have been an actual race against the clock.

E. K. Chambers, the twentieth century authority and a fine Shake-speare scholar, is convinced that the composition of *Romeo and Juliet* closely followed the unhappy termination of a love affair for Shake-speare. If we can determine a candidate for the Shake-speare pedestal who said farewell to a lover about 1590 or 1591, we shall have clue number two.

Edmund Malone, the father of Shake-speare chronology, who probably knew more about the Bard than any other man of the eighteenth and nineteenth centuries, made a first effort in this direction in 1778. Two years later he did a considerable amount of alteration in a revised edition of his first guess at the chronological order of the plays. In 1821, James Boswell, the younger, edited Malone's notes to make a third guess at chronological order, in which there was considerable reversion to the 1778 guess and some wholly new ideas. E. K. Chambers has largely followed Malone; his chronological order is presented in Appendix A in table form under the title of the "1930 Guess." Appendix B is my own "1955 Guess." The "1955 Guess" assigns dates not only to the plays but to the sonnets and the long poems as well.

While dwelling on chronological order, mention should be made of the contribution of Francis Meres. Meres was a graduate of Cambridge who lived in London during 1597 and 1598. In September of 1598 he published *Palladis Tamia: Wits Treasury*. It was a work in praise of a number of poets and playwrights of the period. He called Shake-speare the most excellent of the dramatists for both comedy and tragedy, naming six comedies: *The Two Gentlemen of Verona, The Comedy of Errors, Love's Labour's Lost, Love's Labour's Won, A Midsummer Night's Dream,* and *The Merchant of Venice.* Meres listed six tragedies: *King Richard II, King Richard III, King Henry IV, King John, Titus Adronicus,* and *Romeo and Juliet. Love's Labour's Won* has been identified by Leslie Hotson and others as *Troilus and Cressida.* At least twelve plays had had a London presentation by 1598. We know it is not a complete list; the enumeration was largely the result of the performances that Francis Meres had witnessed over a two-year period. Meres also gave Shake-speare high praise as a poet:

> "As the soule of Euphorbos was thought to live in Pythagoras: so the sweete witte soule of Ovid lives in mellifluous and hony-tongued Shakespeare, witnes his Venus and Adonis, his Lucrece, his sugred Sonnets among his privat friends, etc."

Pythagoras, the sixth century B.C. mathematician and mystic, was a favorite philosopher of the age of Shake-speare. The Elizabethans were intrigued by the hypothesis of Pythagoras that "Number rules the universe." The sixteenth century marked the beginning of the English Renaissance. To believe what the ancient Greeks believed was smart and fashionable. Pythagoras left a profound influence on both Plato and Aristotle, and what Plato and Aristotle took seriously the Elizabethans took seriously. That the power of number's was a popular study may be ascertained by the universal appeal of Dr. John Dee, numerologist, astrologer, and alchemist. Dee was the leading authority in the realm of the magical sciences and was visited by Queen Elizabeth and many of her courtiers.

As has been shown, Sonnet 104 abounds in the rhythm of the number three. The ancients called the number three a perfect number because it was expressive of the beginning, the middle, and the end. The number nine was a mystical number, being thrice three, hence the perfect plural, and represented perfection or completion. As shall be seen in the beginning of the next chapter, the number nine signified perfection and completion for the sagacious Latin poet, Horace.

The Pythagorian Prayer ends thus: ". . . For the divine number begins with the profound, pure unity until it comes to the holy four; then it begets the mother of all, the all-comprising, the all-abounding, the first born, the never-swerving, the never-tiring holy ten, the keyholder of all." Pythagoras thought ten was the most fortunate of numbers. Lucky was he whose Life Cycle Number was ten. Shake-speare demonstrated an indulgence in both the number three and the number ten; if he had a favorite of favorites it was ten. Perhaps ten was his Life Cycle Number. The number ten occurs many times in his writings and often in what might be termed crucial places. Strangely enough, important dates in his literary efforts may be arranged in cycles of ten-year intervals: 1593—1603—1613—1623. 1593 was the date of publication of his first work to be printed, *Venus and Adonis*. Publication of poems and plays went on steadily for a space of ten years and then suddenly stopped in 1603, and for five years not a play, sonnet, or poem was published. During the same five-year interval not a single play was registered with the Company of Stationers until late in the fifth year (November 1607). In 1613 his last play to reach the stage, *King Henry VIII*, was produced. The epilogue to *Henry VIII* has as its first line " 'Tis ten to one this play can never please." The year 1623 is significant for the publication of the First Folio of Shake-speare's Plays. Another cycle of ten-year intervals is 1589—1599—1609. In 1589 the sonnets were completed. In 1599 William Jaggard published the first sonnets to be printed (Sonnets 138 and 144) in the *Passionate Pilgrim*. William Jaggard and Isaac Jaggard, father and son, published the First Play Folio. 1609 is the date of publication of the First Folio of Shake-speare's Sonnets.

Long ago Shake-speare scholarship bogged down at finding plausible explanations for the several Shake-speare mysteries. Edmund Malone sounded the defeatist keynote in his letter to Thomas Perry on December 9, 1802, with this poignant observation: "Everyday produces somewhat about all our old poets, except Shakespeare. No body in his time seems to have written the slightest scrap about him." The orthodox philosophy contends we are up against a stone wall, that the mysteries are destined to remain mysteries. There are two alternate possibilities: The stone wall may be real; on the other hand, the stone wall may crumble to dust if the orthodox time-scale (Chambers, 1930; Malone, 1778, 1780, 1821) should happen to be materially erroneous. We must labor diligently to arrive at a correct time-scale. How are we to know that our time-scale is correct? We shall gain assurance as each problem settles logically into its time-groove.

Chapter III

RIDDLES AND CLUES

"Still, if you shall hereafter find your pen
Stray into poetry, I'd have you then
Try its effect on critic Tarpa's ears
Then on your sire's and mine, and good nine years
Keep it shut closely up in your scrutore
While 'tis unpublished, you can blot and score;
But words once spoken come back nevermore."

Ars Poetica of Horace

History must give many hints as to the real Shake-speare if we could but read history aright. The plays, the poems, and especially the sonnets must abound in signposts to the proper identification if only the art of literary psychology were developed into an all-seeing and all-knowing science. The reason the identity of Shake-speare is shrouded in mystery may very well be that it was planned that way. We should label this plan a deliberate, premeditated stratagem rather than a deliberate hoax, for while the author is in part playing a joke on his audience, the secret of authorship was planned for any number of good and sufficient motives. For such a deliberate, deep-laid deception to have been successful for a period of close to four hundred years would argue that only a few individuals were entrusted with the secret. Without much doubt the "lovely boy" of the sonnets knew Shake-speare's identity; somewhat less certain but still probable is the case for "Mr. W. H." and the "dark lady" of the sonnets. There is a good chance that Christopher Marlowe, Thomas Windebank, Edmund Tylney, and Tylney's nephew, Sir George Buck, knew Shake-speare. Tylney became Master of the Revels on a temporary basis in December of 1578 and received a writ of permanent appointment from Queen Elizabeth on July 29, 1579. Tylney held office until his death on August 20, 1610. Tylney had his nephew appointed as his deputy with reversionary rights to the office secured to the nephew. In

1610 Sir George Buck succeeded his uncle as Master of the Revels and held office until he went mad on March 29, 1622. We wonder what wild tales Sir George told in his madness?

The good sense written by Horace is so timeless as to seem as appropriate today as when it was first expounded in the first century before Christ. Queen Elizabeth was wont to quote Horace more than any other of the ancient poets and no doubt her court reflected her admiration of the great Roman. One of the best known of the works of Horace is the so called *Ars Poetica*. *Ars Poetica* is an epistle to the Pisos Family, Father and Sons, dear friends of Horace. The letter goes into considerable detail on exactly how to write a play. Whoever Shake-speare happened to be, he had the greatest admiration and respect for Horace and his teachings. Horace says:

"The chorus place and function is alway
To prove a busy actor in their play."

Shake-speare echoes in *As You Like It*, act 3, scene 4, when

Rosalind says:

"I'll prove a busy actor in their play."

Horace says:

"Ye who desire to excel, turn
over the Grecian models night and day."

Shake-speare did just that.

Horace says:

"Five acts a play must have, nor more nor less,
To keep the stage and have a marked success."

Every one of Shake-speare's thirty-seven plays has five acts, 'nor more, nor less.'

In 1925, Edward H. Sugden published a compilation called *A Topographical Dictionary to the Works of Shakespeare and His Fellow Dramatists*. In an index to the dictionary are listed the probable dates of the first stage production of each play. Mr. Sugden's probable dates of first stage production have been selected as a guide in our book because it is deemed the best available compilation. A dictionary treatise should be more factual and more scientific than the tracts of biographical writers on Shake-speare, who are by necessity expounding and upholding some theory or other. Sugden's dictionary index gives 1588 as the probable date for the first stage presentation of *Titus Andronicus* and 1589 as the first production of *The Comedy of Errors* and *Love's Labour's Lost.* It is not illogical that Shake-speare followed the GOOD NINE .YEARS KEEP IT SHUT CLOSELY UP IN YOUR SCRUTORE advice of Horace like he followed all the other precepts of Horace. If Shake-speare wrote drama for nine years and then started to put on the stage what he considered the best of the lot, then he started as a playwright in 1579. That 1579 was a most significant year we will discover in due time. You will recall that 1591 has already been selected as the approximate transition date for the end of the immature plays and the beginning of the mature plays. If we proceed at a modest rate of writing from the year 1579, listing the apprentice plays, the simple plays, the experimental plays, and the immature plays between 1579 and 1591 (*The Merry Wives of Windsor* excepted); with the subtle, seasoned, mature, and profound plays after 1591, then we come up with the "1955 Guess" of Appendix B.

A study of Appendix A and Appendix B will establish the fact that without exception the "1955 Guess" has placed the writing of each and every play at an earlier date than the "1930 Guess"; in some instances there is a discrepancy of many years. What advantages has the "1930 Guess" over the "1955 Guess"? The answer is, ever so many advantages. Mr. Chambers is a recognized authority on Shake-speare. The "1930 Guess" makes the natural assumption that all the plays were produced within a short period of time after they were written. What playwright, especially a hungry playwright, and most of them suffered from lack of cash, would voluntarily wait nine months, let alone nine years to produce his first play?

The "1955 Guess" assumes that Shake-speare was a very patient fellow indeed and that he was never a hungry playwright. His contemporary dramatists were often in dire financial straits (except Marlowe who always seemed to be in the money) and were wont to use any writing means to obtain a few pounds including the production of novels, eulogies, pamphlets, and even jokebooks. Several writers penned pleading letters to their patrons for aid. Shake-speare wrote nothing but plays, poems, and sonnets. If he ever wrote a single letter to anyone about anything and signed it with a Shakespearean signature, we have no record of any such letter.

Queen Elizabeth died on March 24, 1603, bringing to a close the brilliant Elizabethan Age and beginning the not so luminous Jacobean Era. The chief difficulties incurred in the "1930 Guess" are brought on by attempting to make Shake-speare a Jacobean playwright. Several of Shake-speare's contemporary writers called upon Shake-speare to eulogize the Great Queen after her death. The public seemed to expect such a tribute as inevitable, yet Shake-speare remained strangely silent. According to E. K. Chambers the only period between 1590 and 1613 in which the great man was completely idle was 1603–4. In the last chapter the point was made that after a steady stream of publication for the ten years (1593–1603), the stream dried up for the next five years (1603–8), when not only was there no publication but not until the very close of the five-year period (November 1607) was a single play registered with the Company of Stationers.

According to the "1930 Guess" the last six plays written by Shake-speare were *Timon of Athens*, *Pericles*, *Cymbeline*, *The Winter's Tale*, *The Tempest*, and *King Henry VIII*. To the most orthodox of writers on Shake-speare, these half-dozen plays compound a paradox. Of the many writers who have had something to say about these plays the most common adjectives used in describing them are *simple*, *apprentice*, *immature*, *mediocre*, *problem plays*, *workshop*, and *experimental*.

One theory contends that Shake-speare suffered a physical and mental breakdown during this period. During such a period of physical and mental illness, we would not expect six indifferent plays; we would expect no plays at all. Another suggestion is that Shake-speare was using a new-type play, the so-called tragi-comedy. Of this theory, E. K. Chambers makes this comment, "The theory that Shakespeare was inspired to write romantic tragi-comedy by the example of Beaumont and Fletcher can hardly be substantiated." Still another theory is that Shake-speare used collaborators on a number of the last six plays. That there were other hands than Shake-speare's in some of these productions seems certain, but such co-authorship suggests several interesting possibilities.

Just what do the critics have to say about the final six plays?

Some representative examples will be quoted. Ashley H. Thorndyke comments on *Cymbeline, The Winter's Tale,* and *The Tempest* thus, ". . . the heroines are not witty. . . ." Of *Cymbeline*
he says, the author ". . . appears to be straining after startling
situations and a complicated denouement, but without much spon-
taneity. At all events, in spite of telling situations, the play is
tedious on the stage." Of *The Tempest*, Thorndyke says, "Yet he
seems to have laboured under various artistic impulses, and the
style is often curiously involved. From his earlier plays he found
examples for the shipwreck, the drunken boors, the talkative old
man, and the youthful lovers; and for some reason he took special
pains to set forth all the marvelous happenings in strict adherence
to Aristotle's unities of time and place."

Thomas Marc Parrott declares *The Tempest* to be perhaps the
simplest of all the Shake-speare plays since *Love's Labour's Lost*
and, further, "It would be absurd to call it great drama; there is no
real dramatic conflict in it; its action is not determined by its inter-
play of characters."

George Bernard Shaw has this to say about *Cymbeline*, "It is
for the most part stagey trash of the lowest melodramatic order, in
parts abominably written, throughout intellectually vulgar, and,
judged by modern intellectual standards, vulgar, foolish, offensive,
indecent, and exasperating beyond all tolerance." Again, ". . .:
in *Cymbeline* and *The Tempest* he troubled himself so little about
it (the art of acting) that he actually writes down the exasperating
clownish interruptions he once denounced; . . ."

H. B. Charlton makes this comment, "*The Tempest* and *Cymbeline* rely too often on the depiction of a mood or on the use of a
convention as a substitute for the fundamental art of characterization. These plays have, of course, their own virtue. But there
could be no clearer evidence of the weakening of Shake-speare's
dramatic genius. For our particular argument, its most manifest
symptom is seen by comparing the heroines of the romances with
those of the mature comedies. To set a Perdita or a Miranda by
the side of a Rosalind or a Viola is to put a slip of girlhood by the
side of women who have grown into the world, become a part of
its fabric and enriched their personality by traffic with affairs and
with other men and women."

William Hazlitt says, "The character of Cleopatra is a masterpiece. What an extreme contrast it affords to Imogen! One would think it almost impossible for the same person to have drawn both." Chambers states this contrast in a similar strain, "The puppet Imogen, set between the puppet Cloten and the puppet Posthumus, may pass for perfection, so long as the danger of comparison with the flesh and blood of Cleopatra or even of Cressida is scrupulously avoided."

Allardyce Nicoll explains, "A third, and more likely, suggestion has of late been gaining support—that the text of *Timon* derives entirely from Shake-speare's pen but that it is no more than a first, and unrevised, copy of a play he never took the trouble to bring to final artistic shape. . . . Although in structure *The Tempest* deviated markedly from the extended canvas of *Pericles*, *Cymbeline*, and *The Winter's Tale*, in fact its planning is not far removed from these. . . . We move into another realm of myth and legend. *Pericles* derives from Hellenistic romance material; *Cymbeline* is set in an almost prehistoric atmosphere; in *The Winter's Tale* the idyllic mingles with the classical; and *The Tempest* is a figment of the imagination." Of *Pericles*, Nicoll relates, "The characters indeed assume an almost visionary quality, so that they stand before us, not so much as symbols, but rather as a dramatic excuse for the presentation of the miraculous; and the action at times is dealt with so summarily as almost to suggest the crudity of an amateur's pen. . . . Is the discovery of the long-lost Thaisa as a 'nun' not the same as the discovery of Æmilia as an 'abbess' in *The Comedy of Errors?*" Nicoll remarks of *Cymbeline*, ". . . and, in a rather strange manner, even motifs from the very early *Titus Andronicus* enter in to take new shape." He also says, "Yet it (*The Winter's Tale*) exhibits precisely the same apparent naïvetes as the others."

With all this evidence at hand, the normal and logical conclusion is that these six immature plays belong chronologically to the first of Shake-speare's dramatic attempts and that for some reason or other they were the last to be made public. Many writers have expostulated this theory. Victor Hugo thought *Pericles* to be Shake-speare's first play. John Dryden has expressed the same idea, "Shakespeare's own Muse her *Pericles* first bore." Samuel Coleridge said in his lectures, "I think Shakespeare's earliest dramatic attempt . . . was *Love's Labour's Lost*. Shortly afterwards

I suppose *Pericles* and certain scenes in *Jeronymo* to have been produced; and in the same epoch, I place *The Winter's Tale* and *Cymbeline* . . . when Shakespeare's celebrity . . . enable him to bring forward the laid by labours of his youth."

Frank Harris saw parallels between *The Winter's Tale* and *Much Ado About Nothing*; between *The Tempest* and *As You Like It*; between *Cymbeline* and *As You Like It*: *Much Ado About Nothing*. According to Harris, "The story of *The Winter's Tale* is taken from *Much Ado*: Hermoine is slandered Hero over again: and *The Tempest* with its story of the two Dukes repeats the theme of *As You Like It*. *Cymbeline*, too, is hardly more than a mixture of the themes of both these earlier comedies: Imogen is slandered like Hero and wanders out into the world like Rosalind." A much more plausible conclusion would be that *The Winter's Tale*, an immature drama, was used for a plot of a later seasoned comedy, *Much Ado About Nothing*. Likewise it would follow that *As You Like It*, perhaps the Bard's finest comedy, was based upon episodes experimentally dealt with in *The Tempest* and in *Cymbeline*.

Shake-speare may have discarded *Cymbeline*, *The Winter's Tale*, and *The Tempest* partly because of this duplication of plots. It would be natural for him to discard *Pericles* as too amateurish to be worthy of the stage. Shake-speare probably never meant these four plays to be acted; he no doubt intended that they be preserved only as examples of his early development. The thought may never have crossed his mind that these four plays could possibly be mistaken for later work. We cannot avoid speculating upon the possibility that Shake-speare was dead prior to 1607. Those to whom he entrusted the manuscripts, after all the good plays were gone and in the absence of any specific instructions to the contrary, would doubtless have given to the public the residue of the master's dramas.

E. K. Chambers saw the similarity of construction and the method of exposition between *The Tempest* and *The Comedy of Errors*: "He reverted to the method of preliminary exposition which he had employed long ago for a similar theme in *The Comedy of Errors*." Why should this reversion be "long ago" when it is much more logical to assume that *The Tempest* and *The Comedy of Errors* are similar plays written in the same period of early dramatic effort? Dover Wilson called *The Tempest*, "a loosely constructed drama, like *The Winter's Tale* and *Pericles*."

The two plays which concern us most out of these half-dozen problem plays are *Timon of Athens* and *The Famous History of the Life of King Henry VIII*, and we have saved them until the last for comment. *Timon of Athens* has been placed as the first play written according to the "1955 Guess." *Timon* may well contain hints about the character of Shake-speare not revealed in other plays, especially since *Timon of Athens* shows clearly the evidence of personal stress and strain. E. K. Chambers says, "Both *King Lear* and *Timon of Athens* seem to show symptoms of mental disturbance."

William Hazlitt describes the play thus, "*Timon of Athens* always appeared to us to be written with as intense a feeling of his subject as any play of Shakespeare. It is one of the few in which he seems to be in earnest throughout, never to trifle nor go out of his way. He does not relax his efforts, nor lose sight of the unity of his design. It is the only play of our author in which spleen is the predominant feeling of the mind. It is as much a satire as a play: and contains some of the finest pieces of invective possible to be conceived, both in the snarling, captious answers of the cynic Apemantus, and in the impassioned and more terrible imprecations of Timon."

Timon of Athens, although in the form of a play in the usual five acts, is actually not a play at all and has little audience appeal; it is an *oration on ingratitude*. While ingratitude is the central theme, jealousy, hatred, and intense loathing also expose their ugly faces. The same hatred and abhorrence of an unfaithful woman which has subtle outcrops in *Timon of Athens* becomes the main treatise of the Dark Lady Sonnets. Was this dual dissertation on hatred aimed at one and the same woman? Is *Cressida* still another portrait of this same female?

Samuel Johnson left to posterity this classification, "The historical dramas are now concluded, of which the two parts of *Henry IV* and *Henry V* are among the happiest of our author's compositions; and *King John, Richard III*, and *Henry VIII* deservedly stand in the second class." Samuel Johnson classified *King Henry VIII* as a second-class history-drama along with two early histories; the inference which can be drawn is that *King Henry VIII*, like

John and *Richard III*, was an early attempt at chronicle-play composition.

Of the six problem plays, only one is sometimes referred to as first-class; and that *The Tempest*. Those who see in *The Tempest* Shake-speare's valediction argue with more enthusiasm than conviction. The great weight of critical opinion declares *The Tempest* to be a simple play, with more weakness than strength. The inferiority of the last six plays of the "1930 Guess" may best be ascertained by a comparison with the six plays immediately preceding the last six; namely *Measure for Measure*, *Othello*, *King Lear*, *Macbeth*, *Anthony and Cleopatra*, and *Coriolanus*. Four of this group are first-class and at least three are masterpieces of the highest dramatic art. Among the final six there is not a single masterpiece and there is only one that dares to seek the appellation of first-class.

Shake-speare's valedictory is in last place on the production line, where the valedictory play should be. *The Famous History of the Life of King Henry VIII* was the last play on the stage and, if we are not mistaken, it was placed last because of Shake-speare's specific instructions. In spite of the allusions to the reign of James I, which we conclude were added at a later date, *King Henry VIII* is an early play. Probably *King Henry VIII* is the first chronicle play Shake-speare attempted since it has many imperfections and leans more heavily upon Raphael Holinshed's *The Chronicles of England, Scotland and Ireland* (*1577*) than is the case for any other history play. Josephine and Allardyce Nicoll state this fact clearly, "It will be found that more of Holinshed's actual wording has been retained in this play than in any other drama. Characterization, episode and dialogue owe directly to the chronicles."

The elaborate title is another indication that the play is early; an immature writer would be more apt to use extravagant language in a title. Yet Shakespeare may have intended the word Famous as a clue to a clue. If Shake-speare left a clue as to his identity, what more reasonable place could he choose than the last speech of his last play upon the stage? E. K. Chambers was puzzled by the position of *Henry VIII* and he expresses the enigma thus, "The reversion to the epic chronicle at the very end of Shake-speare's career is odd." An epic chronicle is history of a kind and what better way could Shake-speare reveal his own history than in a history play?

Henry VIII was first presented on the stage of the Globe Theatre on June 29, 1613. In act 1, scene 4, the stage direction said "Drum and trumpet, chambers discharged." The Globe Theatre caught fire and burned to the ground from the fireworks used in the "chambers discharged." So the play as presented on June 29, 1613 never got beyond the first act. The last speech in the play was never spoken on that date and when we reproduce this last speech for you, it proves to be a disappointment. It is King Henry speaking:

> "Oh lord archbishop!
> Thou hast made me now a man: never before
> This happy child, did I get anything.
> This oracle of comfort has so pleas'd me,
> That, when I am in heaven, I shall desire
> To see what this child does, and praise my Maker.
> I thank ye all. To you, my good lord mayor,
> And your good brethren, I am much beholding;
> I have receiv'd much honour by your presence,
> And ye shall find me thankful. Lead the way, lords:
> Ye must all see the queen, and she must thank ye;
> She will be sick else. This day, no man think
> Has business at his house; for all shall stay:
> This little one shall make a holiday."
>   Exeunt.

But stay, while King Henry gives this above speech as the last speech in the play proper, there is an epilogue. What a strange epilogue! In many ways it sounds like many another epilogue and yet there is a difference; this epilogue is more obscure, more subtle, harder to understand. It seems to mean one thing and at the same time to mean something else quite different. The epilogue to *Henry VIII* is also a riddle. We turn feverishly to the Temple notes; no help here for while there are notes on the prologue to *Henry VIII* there is not a single note on the epilogue. So the reader needs be his own literary detective; when you have solved the riddle of the epilogue you will know the identity of Shake-speare.

EPILOGUE TO KING HENRY VIII

" 'Tis ten to one this play can never please
All that are here: some come to take their ease,
And sleep an act or two: but those, we fear,
We have frighted with our trumpets; so 'tis clear
They'll say 'tis naught: others to hear the city
Abus'd extremely, and to cry 'That's witty!'
Which we have not done neither: that, I fear,
All the expected good we're like to hear
For this play, at this time, is only in
The merciful construction of good women;
For such a one we show'd 'em: if they smile
And say 't will do, I know, within a while
All the best men are ours; for 'tis ill hap
If they hold when their ladies bid 'em clap."

To solve the riddle may take too much research and if you fail
on your first trial remember you have good company. William
Shakspere, the actor, although he lived until 1616, three years
after the first presentation of *Henry VIII*, never solved the riddle.
William Shakspere knowingly helped perpetrate the deception, yet
he was powerless to explain the deception, and in this way he was
not a fraud. William Shakspere died without knowing the identity
of Shake-speare.

Chapter IV

WILLIAM OF STRATFORD AND JOSEPH CONRAD

*"My task which I am trying to achieve is, by
the power of the written word, to make you hear,
to make you feel—it is, before all, to make you see.
That—and no more, and it is everything. If I succeed, you shall find there according to your deserts:
encouragement, consolation, fear, charm—all you
demand and, perhaps, also that glimpse of truth
for which you have forgotten to ask."*

Joseph Conrad

Most of what little contemporary notice exists of Shake-speare comes down from Henry Chettle, printer-publisher turned play-wright. Robert Greene died on September 2, 1592, leaving un-published and perhaps unfinished his *Groats-worth of Wit*. Chet-tle edited Greene's tract. He rewrote *Groats-worth of Wit* in his own handwriting; his excuse for so doing: Greene's handwriting was difficult for printers to read. Chettle denied that he did more than faithfully copy Greene's words, but, since Chettle was under duress to make such a denial, there is no way of knowing whether or not *Groats-worth* is partly his inspiration or the sole product of Greene's art. *Groats-worth of Wit* was published by Henry Chettle in the fall of 1592 and gave to the world the first notice that Shake-speare was a writer or an actor or both. Apparently Robert Greene was convinced that Shake-speare was both an actor and a dramatist. The *Groats-worth of Wit* has this epic bit of advice for three of the University Wits (usually surmised to be addressed to Marlowe, Nashe, and Lodge):

> "Base-minded men all three of you, if by my misery
> you be not warned: for unto none of you (like me) sought
> those burrs to cleave: those Puppets (I mean) that spake
> from our mouths, those antics garnished in our colors. Is

33

it not strange, that I, to whom they all have been behold-
ing, shall (were ye in that case as I am now) be both at
once of them forsaken? Yes, trust them not: for there
is an upstart Crow, beautified with our feathers, that with
his *Tigers Heart Wrapped in Player's Hide,* supposes he
is as well able to bombast out a blank verse as the best of
you: and being an absolute Johannes fac totum, is in his
own conceit the only Shake-scene in the country. Oh, that
I might entreat your rare wits to be employed in more
profitable courses, and let these apes imitate your past ex-
cellence, and never more acquaint them with your admired
inventions."

"Tigers heart wrapped in player's hide" is a parody on the
line from *3 King Henry VI* which reads, "O tiger's heart wrapped
in a woman's hide." *King Henry VI* must have been on the stage
not later than 1592. Greene is accusing Shake-speare of near-
plagiarism. Now the contention has been made that both Marlowe and Greene collaborated with Shake-speare in writing *King
Henry VI.* A. W. Pollard states, "Greene himself must, I think,
go out, as if he had any charge of the appropriation of his own
work to bring he would have brought it much more loudly."

Almost immediately after the publication of *Groats-worth of
Wit* one or more of the nobility (divers of worship) came to Shake-
speare's defense and forced a hasty retraction from Henry Chettle.
On December 8, 1592, Chettle placed *Kind-Harts' Dreame* with
the Stationers' Register. In the epistle to *Kind-Harts' Dreame*
Chettle apologized to Shake-speare:

> "I am as sorry as if the original fault had been my
> fault, because myself have seen his demeanor no less civil
> than he excellent in the qualities he professes: Besides,
> divers of worship have reported his uprightness of deal-
> ing, which argues his honesty, and his facetious grace in
> writing, that approves his Art."

High praise indeed! What manner of man was this Shake-
speare that in 1592 members of the court wasted no time in de-
fending Shake-speare's good name and Shake-speare's writing

ability? George Bernard Shaw wondered "what was the real nature of the mysterious restraint" that kept Elizabeth and James I from censoring Shake-speare's ever so frank treatment of royalty in his history plays.

That Shake-speare was no ordinary dramatist may be presumed from his complete omission from *Henslowe's Diary*. Philip Henslowe, manager of many London theatres, including the Rose, Fortune, Swan, Hope, and Newington Butts, bought plays from nearly every dramatist of the times. He kept a detailed account book of these transactions, including authors and names of plays, for over two decades from February 17, 1592. Most of these playwrights wrote in *Henslowe's Diary* as well as signed their names to the account records, but there is not a scrap about Shake-speare or any one of his plays. To say that Shake-speare moved in a charmed circle is putting it mildly.

Nathaniel Holmes observed, "And soon after the death of Elizabeth, in 1603, this same Chettle, silenced before, but evidently by no means satisfied, noticed that, among many tributes to the virtues of the late Queen, none came from William Shake-speare, ventured to break out anew in these lines:

'Nor doth the silver-tongued Melicert
Drop from his honied muse one sable tear,
To mourn her death that graced his desert,
And to his laies open'd her royall eare:
Shepheard, remember our Elizabeth,
And sing her rape, done by the Tarquin, Death.'

Mourning Garment, 1603."

The first two recorded facts in the life of William Shakspere occur eighteen years apart. Both records are in Latin. The first records his baptism, "1564, April 26, Gulielmus, filius Johannes Shakspere." The second was a marriage license issued November 27, 1582, "item, eodem die similis emanavit licencia inter Wm. Shaxpere et Annum Whateley de Temple Grafton."

Temple Grafton was a town a few miles from Stratford. Who Anne Whateley was we do not know. William married Anne Hathaway of Stratford a few days later. Early biographers of William Shakspere were able to argue convincingly that Anne

Whateley and Anne Hathaway were one and the same person. Lately there has been a tendency for the authorities on the subject to conclude that William was romantically involved with two women, each seeking the same husband, a not uncommon occurrence in that or any other century. If so, Anne Hathaway, eight years older than William, had the better claim on him, for she was pregnant. Six months later, in May 1583, a daughter was born and baptized Susanna. Early in 1585, twins were born to the William Shaksperes, a boy and a girl, and were named Hamnet and Judith, after family friends, Hamnet Sadler and his wife, Judith. At the age of twenty, William had a wife and three children. At this date William Shakspere's future may have appeared happy, even rosy and joyous, but it did not promise an exciting life for the busy husband and father, much less world fame.

Richard Shakspere, William's grandfather, was a tenant of an old, established, respected family named Arden. The Arden daughter, Mary, married John, the son of her father's tenant. John and William appear to have been good-looking men. Father and son were ambitious, sociable, law-minded and, at least in John's case, civic-minded, for John was at one time a bailiff and for some years was a member of the town council. John was able to reach upward in securing a wife, and we have no reason to believe that Anne Hathaway was not William's social equal. Their marriage may have been entirely satisfactory in spite of the difference in their ages.

If you were to journey to Stratford a guide would show you the desk in the grammar school where William sat, yet we do not possess a single fact about his early life and education beyond the record of his baptism. William was the third child to be born to John and Mary Shakspere. The first two were girls and both died soon after their birth. Since William was baptized on April 26, 1564, it has been deduced that he was born April 21st or 22nd. Stratford had a good grammar school, and since John was the kind of father who would be ambitious for the schooling of his bright son, he may have encouraged William to finish the full course of instruction in the Stratford Grammar School. The custom of the times was to apprentice a lad at about the age of thirteen for a total of seven years. Upon reaching his majority the young man would have served his apprenticeship and be ready to become a craftsman at his chosen trade. Whether William learned to make gloves (his father's vocation), was a wool apprentice, or a butcher's helper, we do not know. The most popular legend, that he followed the butcher's trade, has no real grounds to support it.

In the year 1587 there is a record of a negotiation in which the assent of William Shakspere was necessary for a conveyance at Stratford. That is the last record of the young man until the middle of 1592, when from Robert Greene's *Groats-worth of Wit* we know that William was a successful actor on the London stage and had powerful friends at court, ready to defend his honor and integrity as a writer of plays. How he got to London, why he went to London, when he went to London, how he learned to act, we do not know. The five-year period, 1587–92, is a void. 1587–92 joins 1564–82 to make 23 blank years out of a total of 28.

Every Shakespearean authority (authority is invariably spelled o-r-t-h-o-d-o-x) will tell you that William Shakspere, the actor, and Shake-speare, the dramatist and poet, are one and the same person. The authorities may be right and then again they may be wrong; it's a moot question. If William Shakspere, the actor, wrote the thirty-seven plays, the 154 sonnets, the two long poems and the shorter poems which comprise Shake-speare's works, then he rode a literary rocket at supersonic speed to stratospheric fame. We are awestruck at such a display of genius.

Only one other English writer has come close to conquering such a vast multitude of obstacles as friend William Shakspere. Joseph Conrad, although a native of an inland country, spent all his youth at sea. Utterly ignorant of a word of English at twenty years of age, he became not only a great English novelist but developed a new and powerful style of English composition. We will find it illuminating both to compare and to contrast the rise of William Shakspere and the rise of Joseph Conrad.

In 1893 John Galsworthy took passage on a sailing vessel from Australia to Capetown on his trip around the world. He became acquainted with the black-bearded first mate, Josef Teodor Konrad Korzeniowski from Poland, who had become a naturalized English citizen in 1886 and had changed his name to Joseph Conrad. The two men became fast friends.

Joseph's father was a man of letters. Joseph was carefully

educated by private tutors. He learned to read and write French almost as well as Polish. Joseph read widely, including translations of Shake-speare and Dickens. Sea stories excited his imagination, and at seventeen he joined the French merchant marine. At the age of twenty-two he knew a few words of English and was a sailor in the English merchant fleet. Joseph Conrad, in finding out about life, became a sailor, a smuggler, and a gun-runner. What were the extracurricular activities of William? In his early life he dealt in gloves or wool or meat. In later life he bought and sold property, engaged in numerous lawsuits (sometimes over trifling sums of money), and worried about which of his relatives would inherit the various items of his real and personal property—which personal property listed not a single manuscript or other writing and not a single book of any kind.

In his middle life Shakspere was either a fair or a good actor, but apparently was never good enough to achieve top billing on any play program. When did William have his adventures? The tale that William was dodging a jail sentence for deer-stealing in the park of Sir Thomas Lucy of Cherlecot, and therefore fled from Stratford to London, cannot be true because Sir Thomas Lucy did not acquire the deer park until much later. When did William become an authority on love, an authority on women, an authority on the seven seas, an authority on war and military tactics, an authority on politics, history, law, and religion? When did he learn Spanish, French, and Italian?

Joseph Conrad worked on his first novel, *Almayer's Folly*, for five years, 1889 to 1894, before he finished it. This first work he managed to have published, but it brought him no recognition by the public even though he had the backing of such men as Henry James, Stephen Crane, John Galsworthy, and Ford Madox Ford. Many novels and a host of short stories later, in 1913, twenty-four years after he had begun to write, he began to receive some public acclaim. Conrad's fifteenth published volume was his first best-seller. William served no such long, hard rise to literary fame. William started to write plays, we are told ("1930 Guess"), about 1590 or 1591, yet by mid-1592 he had written and produced *1 Henry VI*, *2 Henry VI*, and *3 Henry VI*, and he was well on his way toward becoming a mature playwright; his plays were well received on the London stage and he had excited the envy of a mature dramatist, Robert Greene. What kind of assistance and influence are we to suppose must have been back of the Man from Stratford to push him to prominence in one or two years? If the "1930 Guess" is correct, Christopher Marlowe, at the height of his fame and literary power and never in need of money, consented to collaborate on *Henry VI* with the freshman playwright from the provinces. The proposition is absurd, especially so because Marlowe lacked a sense of humor. The authorities also say that it is impossible that a mature play such as *Romeo and Juliet* could have been written as early as 1591. Therefore, in spite of the clear-cut evidence of the earthquake dating, which they argue somehow does not mean what it says, they place the date of composition for *Romeo and Juliet* as 1595.

The "1930 Guess" when combined with the Sugden Table of first production dates informs us blandly that *The Comedy of Errors* and *The Two Gentlemen of Verona* were written three or four years after they first appeared on the stage. Also that *Titus Adronicus, Love's Labour's Lost,* and *King John* were written five or six years after their first stage appearance.

Joseph Conrad was still writing in 1924, the year of his death; he was in his late sixties. The last play of Shake-speare was written no later than 1611. In 1611 William was only forty-seven; he lived for five more years, yet wrote not another line. Joseph Conrad, like most writers, was enthusiastic about literary art. There is much evidence that William of Stratford did not like to write. Where are William's letters to his friends, to his fellow actors, and to his fellow poets? What remains to posterity of William Shakspere's handwriting? The only holographic material in existence which is indisputable consists of six signatures—one on a deposition in 1612, two on a conveyance and mortgage in 1613, and three on his will. As nearly as one can decipher the signatures, he wrote his name SHAKSPERE. In no instance did he write it SHAKESPEARE. Hamnet, William Shakspere's only son, died in 1596. What must have been a heavy grief finds no expression in any of the Shake-speare writings; no sonnet, no poem, no dedication, nothing. Some authorities try to establish some reference to Hamnet in the grief of Constance at the death of her son Arthur, in *King John*; yet Sugden lists *King John* as on the stage in 1591. Shake-speare had no praise for Elizabeth when she died: one critic states that he is the only English poet who did not eulogize the dead queen.

In all fairness it must be admitted—the other candidates for the throne of Shake-speare suffer even more than William from the time-scale. There is nothing new about the theory that SHAKE-SPEARE is a nom de plume. The first book to suggest that William Shakspere, the actor, and Shake-speare, the writer, were two different men was written by Herbert Lawrence in 1769 and entitled *The Life and Adventures of Commonsense: an Historical Allegory.* Lawrence came up with a logical contender for Shake-speare in the person of Sir Francis Bacon (1561–1626), whose life span slightly overlaps that of William of Stratford. In the nearly two centuries that have elapsed since Lawrence's book, Bacon shows no sign of ever winning the championship. For one thing, why did Francis Bacon fail to write any plays in the fifteen-year stretch from 1611 to 1626? Almost without exception, the other challengers face the same difficulty. Those who put forward the claims of William Stanley, sixth Earl of Derby (1561–1642) must explain thirty-one years of non-production. Sir Walter Raleigh lived for seven years after 1611 (1552–1618), while the Countess of Pembroke lived for ten years after 1611 (1561–1621). Roger Manners, 1576–1612, fifth Earl of Rutland, was born a bit too late to be taken seriously.

In connection with the subject of the immaturity of the last six plays of the "1930 Guess," the conjecture was made that Shake-speare might have died sometime prior to 1607. Therefore, Edward de Vere, 17th Earl of Oxford (1550–1604), cannot be ruled out merely because of his death in 1604. We know a great deal about the life of De Vere, and, while he was a writer, he was much too ordinary a person to ever measure up to the description of "myriad-minded." Furthermore, he was anti-Leicester, anti-Essex, and anti-Southampton; whereas we have ample evidence that Shake-speare was pro-Leicester, pro-Essex, and pro-Southampton. Oxford was a Catholic and it is difficult for one to imagine a Catholic writing *King John.*

Sir Edward Dyer (1543–1607) was mentioned by Francis Meres in 1598 as "famous for elegy." In 1589 Puttenham pronounced him to be "for elegy most sweet, solemn and of high conceit." Critics in the seventeenth century, in gathering together his poetic works, "were at a loss to know on what work his fame rested." Dyer does not fit either the "universal genius" test nor the "myriad-minded" test and must be eliminated.

The authorities on Shakspere biography at some point or other remind their readers that in the sixteenth century a man in his forties was in a state of tottering antiquity. Of William's six rivals who are chronological possibilities—Bacon, Raleigh, Pembroke, Stanley, De Vere, and Dyer—the oldest died at eighty-one, the youngest at fifty-four, with the average age at death sixty-five. No telling how long Sir Walter Raleigh would have lived if he had not been deprived of his head. There is not a shred of evidence against the hypothesis that William Shakspere was at the height of his physical and mental powers in his forties.

Since William fits the time-scale as well as if not better than his rivals, could he be our "myriad-minded" poet in addition to being an actor? We will let you be the judge. We know William Shakspere wrote one bit of poetry, the epitaph on his tombstone. We will present this poem and underneath it place one of Shakespeare's early sonnets and let you compare the philosophy, depth of thought, beauty and literary style of each to see if you think the same man could possibly have written both.

> "Good friend, for Jesus sake forbear
> To dig the dust enclosed here;
> Blest be the man who spares these stones,
> And curst be he that moves my bones.

> William Shakspere"

Sonnet 18

> "Shall I compare thee to a summer's day?
> Thou art more lovely and more temperate:
> Rough winds do shake the darling buds of May,
> And summer's lease hath all too short a date:
> Sometimes too hot the eye of heaven shines,
> And often is his gold complexion dimm'd;
> And every fair from fair sometimes declines,
> By chance of nature's changing course untrimm'd;

But thy eternal summer shall not fade,
Nor lose possession of that fair thou ow'st,
Nor shall death brag thou wander'st in his shade,
When in eternal lines of time thou grow'st;
So long as men can breathe, or eyes can see,
So long lives this, and this gives life to thee."

                                        Shake-speare

Thinking over the evidence furnished by the events of the late years of William Shakspere—his business dealings, his lawsuits, and especially of the detailed provisions of his famous will in which he forgot to mention his wife, and interlined the gift of the second-best bed to Mrs. Shakspere as an afterthought—we know to whom he is to be compared. William of Stratford is very like Soames Forsythe, the hero and "Man of Property" in the two trilogies of John Galsworthy.

If we were to lay aside the time-scale for the time being and merely look for contemporary authors capable of being Shake-speare, we would not include Sir Francis Bacon. He was a celebrated writer and we do not doubt his genius. He wrote good prose but uninspiring poetry, and his genius was of another sort. The two genii were poles apart in their thinking. In his first seventeen sonnets, in *All's Well That Ends Well,* and in many other instances Shake-speare is a strong defender and supporter of the institution of matrimony. In Bacon's essay *On Marriage and Single Life* he expounds his philosophy, "He that hath Wife and Children, hath given Hostages to Fortune; for they are Impediments to great Enterprises, either of Virtue or Mischief."

Christopher Marlowe, Robert Greene, Sir Walter Raleigh, and the Countess of Pembroke were all writers of distinction. Early death eliminated Greene and Marlowe. Those who see the period of composition of the last six plays of the "1930 Guess" (1607–11) as a period of mental depression should like Sir Walter Raleigh as a candidate, for that gentleman was under King James' sentence of death and/or life imprisonment from 1603 to 1618.

While it seems probable that William Shakspere, the actor, possessed a fair amount of education as well as a high order of native intelligence, there is always the possibility that William was a male Pygmalion sans the romantic angle. The fact that his parents were probably both illiterate does not seem especially significant, but the certainty that his younger daughter, Judith, could not read or write makes one wonder. Then there are those six chicken scratches, the six signatures of William Shakspere which comprise the sum-total of his handwriting in existence. I have highly intelligent friends whose handwriting is almost as atrocious as that of Shakspere, but in the age of the typewriter penmanship has become somewhat of a lost art. Not so in the sixteenth century and especially not for a playwright whose writing scores of other people had to be able to read accurately. An Elizabethan learning penmanship in his middle twenties might well have had such a signature as indicated by the six scrawls.

The idle rumor that William started his career in dramatics by holding the carriage horses of the ladies and gentlemen in attendance at a London theatre is just another of those unfounded legends which have no basis of fact. This particular legend seems to be among the silliest, for who can imagine an ambitious husband and father of three leaving Stratford, his family, his friends, his home, and his good trade to become a groom? If William became stagestruck from watching the Stratford performances of a band of traveling players and went to London all fired up to speak somebody's lines by any means and manner that offered itself, it is the one and only time that we find Shakspere playing the cards of life except very close to his waistcoat.

There must have been a good reason back of Shakspere's journey to the metropolis. Malone thought he might have left Stratford with one of the traveling companies of players. Ivor Brown has surmised which company transported William: "Perhaps 1587 was the deciding date. The Queen's Men, with Tarleton and Kemp as Chief Clowns, were in Warwickshire at midsummer. This was the company he was later to serve and to grace." We know Shakspere was with the Lord Chamberlain's Men in 1594. Exactly what company or companies made use of his services before 1594 is debatable. The failure of *Henslowe's Diary* to mention Shake-speare (or Shakspere), or any of the plays, certainly is evidence that the dramatist did not spread his plays, but limited them to a single outlet. Ivor Brown seems certain of this: ". . . for he is the only one of the four who did not shift about from company to company but maintained his close association with a single acting troupe for more than 20 years."

Agreed that the most probable road to London was that William joined a traveling company at Stratford and made the journey with that company, still there looms that toughest of questions: WHY? Why did he want to become an actor, and why did the Queen's Men, or whatever company it was, desire to enroll him as one of their number? Think back over what little we know about William of Stratford, and the inference that he became an actor for the sake of a sum of money is a reasonable conjecture. What asset did William have that would make the Queen's Men offer him a sum of money? He had his name, Shakspere.

Now, if William had no particular interest in the theatre but the monetary return, a single sum of money might take him to London but it would not assure that he would stay there. An actor's salary plus the guarantee of a considerable sum of cash at the termination of a specified long term of service would be the logical contract. The ten-year interval crops up again. 1587 is a probable date for his commencement as an actor. There is a rumor to the effect that the Earl of Southampton paid William the sum of a thousand pounds in the mid-nineties. The sum might have been exaggerated and the donor might not have been Southampton. We do know that in 1597 Shakspere paid off his father's debts and bought New Place, the largest dwelling in Stratford, and in the next few years expended considerable sums of money repairing New Place. Furthermore William was generally more active in Stratford than in London from 1597 on. He was involved in a considerable number of Warwickshire lawsuits, for one thing. William may have spent no more than ten years in London and, save for periodic business trips to the city, may have reverted to a permanent Stratford residence from 1597 until his death.

If Shake-speare was a pen name adopted before 1587, and the manager of the Queen's Men was empowered to hire any potential actor from the provinces with a name similar to Shake-speare, then the nom de plume was no mere whim but an appropriate word-picture highly descriptive of the Bard. The writer's ghost-actor had to be from the provinces in order to obscure his roots. A stand-in from London would not do, for his family and background would be "a motley to the view." Shake-speare is the combination of a verb and a noun; is a complete sentence, and conveys a complete thought or word-picture. Who in all history is best described by the word-picture Shake-speare?

Chapter V

THE DEDICATIONS

"This England never did, nor never shall,
Lie at the proud foot of a conqueror,
But when it first did help to wound itself.
Now these her princes are come home again,
Come the three corners of the world in arms,
And we shall shock them. Nought shall make us rue,
If England to itself do rest but true."

King John

There were only two formal, personal dedications made by Shake-speare, one each to the two long poems, published in 1593 and 1594, and both addressed to the Earl of Southampton, Henry Wriothesly. The two formal dedications were conventional (but misleading); they were cast in the same mold as many another Elizabethan dedication. Some critics have wondered why Shake-speare never again dedicated anything to Southampton. Alfred Harbage has marvelled that, ". . . he did less dedicating than almost any other writer of his time . . ."

The real dedications are internal and are contained in the history plays—a dedication to England, a dedication to be "The Defender of the Faith of Order Against Disorder," and a dedication to his Queen. The finest expression of Shake-speare's devotion to England, of his love and patriotic fervor for his native land, is quoted above and consists of the last seven lines of *The Life and Death of King John.*

We should be accustomed to the figure ten by this time, so that there should be but little surprise that of the thirty-seven plays there are ten histories and ten tragedies. A half-dozen of the seventeen plays listed as comedies should perhaps be classified as tragicomedies since these six have elements of tragedy but lack a tragic conclusion. Shake-speare's natural element was comedy and his *As You Like It* and *Twelfth Night* may some day rank as high as *Lear*, *Hamlet*, and *Macbeth*. Yet it was neither comedy nor tragedy with which Shake-speare was principally concerned; his primary interest was in the history plays. Marlowe wrote only one history play *Edward II*; Shake-speare wrote ten. Marlowe selected the story of King Edward II for its high tragic episodes. His purpose was not to teach history. Shake-speare's epic chronicle themes instructed the English in their glorious but turbulent past. The tragic elements of the Shake-speare history plays were important but not all-important as they were with Marlowe in *Edward II*.

The most puzzling play of all and one that defies classification is *Troilus and Cressida*, for there is no resolution of the dramatic conflict at the conclusion of act five; the action is left hanging in mid-air. Yet, strangely enough, *Troilus and Cressida* is the play most concerned with the order-disorder antithesis: Ulysses speaks:

> "O! when degree is shak'd,
> Which is the ladder to all high designs,
> The enterprise is sick. How could communities,
> Degrees in schools, and brotherhoods in cities,
> Peaceful commerce from dividable shores,
> The primogenitive and due of birth,
> Prerogative of age, crowns, sceptres, laurels,
> But by degree, stand in authentic place?
> Take but degree away, untune that string,
> And, hark! what discord follows; each thing meets
> In mere oppugnancy: the bounded waters
> Should lift their bosoms higher than the shores,
> And make a sop of all this solid globe:
> Strength should be lord of imbecility,
> And the rude son should strike his father dead:
> Force should be right; or rather right and wrong,
> Between whose endless jar justice resides,
> Should lose their names, and so should justice too.
> Then every thing includes itself in power,
> Power into will, will into appetite;
> And appetite, an universal wolf,
> So doubly seconded with will and power,
> Must make perforce an universal prey,
> And last eat up himself."

In *Troilus and Cressida* the crux of all Shake-speare's philosophy, the purpose of the thirty-seven plays, the personal dedication to point out the ways of order and the ways of disorder, is summed up in a single line from the lips of Cassandra, the prophetess:

"IT IS THE PURPOSE THAT MAKES STRONG THE VOW; . . ."

Troilus and Cressida could be called a prelude or a prologue to all of the history plays and as such the suspended ending (illustrative of Negative Capability) would be more understandable.

Nine of the ten history plays constitute a unitized whole by presenting the entire historical record of the War of the Roses and its immediate aftermath. The fifteenth century was for the English people a century of civil strife. Order was not to come until Lancaster had married York and peace was not to heal England until Providence had produced a strong monarch in the person of a granddaughter of the Lancaster-York fusion. The nine plays describe the reigns of the successive kings, Richard II, Henry IV (Bolingbroke), Henry V, Henry VI, Edward IV, Edward V, Richard III, Henry VII, and Henry VIII, and end with the birth and baptism of Elizabeth Tudor. The Edwards are not in the title of any play, although *3 Henry VI* might have been titled *Edward IV*. Henry VII, after his appearance in the play, *Richard III*, is no longer suitable dramatic material. His reign was devoted to merchant pursuits, to exacting revenues for a war upon which he refrained from embarking, and to building up the English navy; all admirable enterprises but not conducive to order-disorder dramatization; hence no play called *Henry VII*.

Nicholas Copernicus (1473–1543), the Polish astronomer, shortly before his death announced the theory that the sun was the center of our solar system around which the earth and other planets revolved. Sixteenth century England all but ignored the Copernican system. Clearly Shake-speare adhered to the old Ptolemaic system. According to Claudius Ptolemy, the second century Alexandrian astronomer, the earth was the central body of the universe around which the sun, the planets, and all other heavenly bodies revolved.

The order-disorder theory of social philosophy was a natural adjunct to the Ptolemaic system. Below man were the animals, below the animals were the plants, and below the plants were the rocks. Above man the angels held sway to be in turn ruled by the archangels; at the top, ruling all, was God. Within each classification each member had his appointed place. In human society each man had his established position, high or low. The King was the anointed of God and was God's representative on earth (the Divine Right of Kings was accepted in all seriousness). The War of the Roses, Shake-speare related in his history plays, was the result of God's anger. The grief and heartache of civil war was the natural sequel to the disorder generated when Bolingbroke forced the abdication of God's appointee, Richard II. The moral: the established order is sacred and cannot be disturbed without disastrous consequences.

The play, *Henry VIII*, varies slightly from fact, most significantly in allowing Catherine of Aragon to die before Elizabeth is born. As a whole the nine plays follow history very closely. True, the critics are bothered by Shake-speare's portrayal of Richard III as the embodiment of total evil; by the riotous youth of Prince Hal; by King Henry V's renunciation of the friends of his careless days as Prince, and by the libels on the character of Joan of Arc. Nevertheless, Shake-speare is following Holinshed's *Chronicles* on these episodes almost to the letter, except in the delineation of the character of Richard, on which exception we will comment in a later chapter.

King John, the one history play not related to the War of the Roses, is unique in being more fable than fact. This epic chronicle could be thought of as an appeal to patriotism from the beginning and as reaching a climax of super-patriotic expression in the last seven lines. These last seven lines are uttered by the lone descendant of the warrior-king, Richard, Coeur de Lion. Richard's bastard son, Philip, knighted Sir Richard and Plantagenet by King John, enriches the play by giving to John a taller stature than he otherwise would have and by the fulfillment of patriotic justice by avenging his father. The Bastard's philosophy of expediency might echo a similar standard in Shake-speare. Philip tells his mother:

"Some sins do bear their privilege on earth,
And so doth yours, your fault was not your folly: . . ."

King John's defiance of Pandulph, cardinal of Milan and legate of Pope Innocent, in the face of certain excommunication as related in the play, might be looked upon as a historic precedent for the church-state schism engineered by Henry VIII and Elizabeth. Also, it might be as close as we will ever come to a summation of Shake-speare's ecclesiastic polity:

> "Though you and all the kings of Christendom
> Are led so grossly by this meddling priest,
> Dreading the curse that money may buy out;
> And by the merit of vile gold, dross, dust,
> Purchase corrupted pardon of a man,
> Who in that sale sells pardon from himself;
> Though you and all the rest so grossly led,
> This juggling witchcraft with revenue cherish,
> Yet I alone, alone do me oppose
> Against the pope and count his friends my foes."

The play, *King John*, varies widely from recorded history, so that the Elizabethan audience could be instructed in expedient solutions to Elizabethan political problems. Actually, John defied the pope only at a distance and when Pandulph came to court, the King in abject submission presented the legate with the English crown, which Pandulph kept for five days (not five minutes as in the play). In the play, Arthur dies by accident, and the several historic years that elapse between the death of Arthur and the death of John is shortened to a matter of hours in the interest of poetic justice. The modern age remembers the reign of John principally for the signing of the Magna Charta and the Charta de Foresta. The play makes no mention of the Magna Charta: the inference may be drawn that Shake-speare had no particular sympathy for democratic milestones.

A whole host of both major and minor discrepancies exist between history and the play and are described in detail in Campbell's "Shakespeare's Histories." Lily B. Campbell views the play of *King John* as Elizabethan political propaganda almost in its entirety. Perhaps the most striking parallel is the speech of John to Hubert, which might very well be the apology of Elizabeth for the execution of Mary, Queen of Scots:

> "It is the curse of kings to be attended
> By slaves that take their humors for a warrant
> To break within the bloody house of life,

And on the winking of authority
To understand a law, to know the meaning
Of dangerous majesty when perchance it frowns
More upon humour than advis'd respect."

The old theory alleged that Shake-speare wrote simply and solely to please his audience. Since 1936 when A. O. Lovejoy published "The Great Chain of Being" with its order-disorder antithesis, we have a much clearer understanding of the fundamental motivations of the Elizabethans. The feeling has been growing that Shake-speare's purpose was to instruct his public quite as much as to amuse them. The play, *King John*, is a case in point. The extensive perversion of historic fact in *King John* called for painstaking manipulation; the playwright was in dead earnest when he reintegrated the actions of a weak king into strong political ammunition. In 1952 Allardyce Nicoll said, "Until recently, there has been a tendency to think of Shakespeare, the dramatist, carelessly picking up some plot or other from a casually perused volume and hastening to mould it into play form. Now, we are coming more and more to believe that he took far greater pains with his preparatory planning than had hitherto been supposed. Quite clearly, he read much more than Holinshed's *Chronicles* when he was writing the history plays, and even when we approach the romances we catch curious glimpses of extended explorations into source material . . . , enough remains to warrant the assumption that he was easily familiar with Latin, French and Italian, that he frequently took the trouble to examine several renderings of a story before he sat down to write."

In 1951, George Duthie commented, "When he wrote his various history plays Shakespeare was not interested merely in chronicling events that had taken place in the past. He was doing that, of course; but his view of history (and it was not peculiar to him) was that past events have a vital significance for the present and the future. . . . Now, of course, patriotism is essentially consonant with the order scheme."

Nicoll found a deep significance in *Henry VIII*, "If we seek for the core of the play we find in it an almost indefinable impression of the mysterious ways of God. We sit spectators of intrigue and the effects of ambition, of confused purposes and selfish affections, and yet somehow out of all this dark and troubled world a miracle

is born, the girl-child who is named Elizabeth." In the last act of
Henry VIII Shake-speare renders his dedication to his Queen
through the prophetic speech of Archbishop Cranmer:

> ". . . All princely graces
> That mould up such a mighty piece as this is
> With all the virtues that attend the good,
> Shall still be doubled on her; truth shall nurse her;
> Holy and heavenly thoughts still counsel her;
> She shall be lov'd and fear'd; her own shall bless her;
> Her foes shake like a field of beaten corn,
> And hang their heads with sorrow; good grows with her.
> In her days every man shall eat in safety
> Under his own vine what he plants; and sing
> The merry songs of peace to all his neighbors.
> God shall be truly known; and those about her
> From her shall read the perfect ways of honour,
> And by those claim their greatness, not by blood."

Elizabeth Tudor had a temper to match her red hair. If you
were a courtier and smiled too broadly at a blonde-in-waiting, you
might be summarily dismissed from the royal presence for a time,
for Elizabeth was a normal woman and as a normal woman she
liked men. She liked the flashing eye and the flattery of men. If
your eye wandered from the Queen and your flattery beat on another pearly ear, Elizabeth could give a sterling performance as a
jealous female. That fiery temper of Good Queen Bess never
really got out of hand or at least it was under proper control when
she was dealing with important matters, whether state problems or
personal problems. Elizabeth thought like a man if by thinking
like a man you mean she possessed a keen, analytical mind which
held sway over her emotions. She could outtalk and outthink each
and every one of her advisers on the Privy Council and she was at
least a match for if not the superior in diplomacy of the many,
many foreign ministers and marriage ambassadors who came to the
English Court.

She was a scholar all her life. At the age when most girls play
with dolls, Elizabeth wrote letters in English, French, and Latin,
containing picturesque similes and metaphors. Even as Queen she
continued to read the classics several hours a day. Roger Ascham,

foremost teacher of his day and tutor to Elizabeth, stated, "It is your shame (I speak to you all, you young gentlemen of England) that one maid should go beyond you all in excellency of learning and knowledge of divers tongues. Point forth six of the best given gentlemen of this court, and all they together show not so much good will, spend not so much time, bestow not so many hours, daily, orderly and constantly, for the increase of learning and knowledge as doth the Queen's majesty herself. Yea, I believe that, beside her perfect readiness in Latin, Italian, French and Spanish, she readeth here at Windsor more Greek every day than some prebendary of this church doth Latin in a whole week."

We gain a clear and illuminating picture of the Good Queen in 1597, six years prior to her death. Elizabeth's Court was gathered to hear what was anticipated to be a flattering and complimentary message to Elizabeth from Paulus Jaline, the Ambassador from Poland. Instead, the Ambassador made threats that his master would punish her if she did not comply with his demands forthwith. It was the Lord Chancellor's place to reply to such an affront but he was not allowed to make a beginning. Elizabeth leaped from the throne, thrust aside the Lord Chancellor and broke out in the following extempore rejoinder, in Latin:

"I look for an Embassy: but you have brought a complaint to me. I understood by your letters that you were a legate, but I find a herald. Never in my life have I heard such an oration. I marvel at so great and such unaccustomed boldness in a public assembly. Neither do I think if your King were present, that he would say so much. But if by chance he did commit any such thing to your charge (which I surely must doubt) this is the reason: That where the King is young, and not by blood, but by election, and newly elected, he does not so perfectly understand the course of dealing in such businesses with other Princes, which either his ancestors have observed with us, or perhaps others will observe that afterward shall succeed in his place. For your part you seem to me to have read many books, but not to have come to the book of Princes, but altogether to be ignorant what is observed between Kings. But were it not your place you hold, to have so public an imputation thrown upon our justice, which as yet never failed, we would answer this audacity of yours in another style. And for the particulars of your negotiations, we will appoint some of our council to confer with you, to see upon what grounds this clamour of yours has its foundation; In the meantime, farewell, and be quiet."

After the astonished Ambassador had hurriedly departed, Elizabeth burst out laughing and said, "God's death, my Lords! but I have been enforced this day to scour up my old Latin that hath lain long rusting."

In 1593 and 1594 the Queen's favorite was the young, dashing Earl of Southampton. Shake-speare reached high for a patron for the only two external dedications he ever made. The 1593 dedication to *Venus and Adonis* reads as follows:

"To The

RIGHT HONOURABLE HENRY WRIOTHESLY,

Earl of Southampton, and Baron
of Tichfield

Right Honourable,

I know not how I shall offend in dedicating my unpolished lines to your lordship, nor how the world will censure me for choosing so strong a prop to support so weak a burden: only if your honour seem but pleased, I account myself highly praised, and vow to take advantage of all idle hours, till I have honoured you with some graver labour. But if the first heir of my invention prove deformed, I shall be sorry it had so noble a godfather, and never after ear so barren a land, for fear it yield me still so bad a harvest. I leave it to your honourable survey, and your honour to your heart's content: which I wish may always answer your own wish and the world's hopeful expectation.

Your honour's in all duty,
William Shakespeare"

Why is this dedication misleading? The sonnets, Shake-speare's finest poetic expression, were written about 1586–89, according to

Leslie Hotson. *Venus and Adonis* is youthful poetry, no authority claims any more merit for it. Shake-speare himself calls it "the first heir of my invention." Clearly it must have been written a number of years before 1586. *The Rape of Lucrece* published in 1594 with the second and last external dedication Shake-speare was to make, is little better in quality than *Venus and Adonis*. William Hazlitt makes this comment: "The two poems of *Venus and Adonis* and of *Tarquin and Lucrece* appear to us a couple of ice-houses. They are about as hard, as glittering, and as cold. The author seems all the time to be thinking of his verses and not his subject, . . ." Mr. Hotson considers Mr. Hazlitt's judgment harsh, but admits the two long poems show "striking inferiority to the profound and masterful work" of the sonnets. Still, Mr. Hotson views the two long poems as written after the sonnets and that "The answer must lie in the kind of market for which they were prepared." Realism would be better served by placing the composition of *Venus* and *Lucrece* at about 1583 and 1584, respectively. When Shake-speare says to Southampton, "and vow to take advantage of all idle hours, till I have honoured you with some graver labour," he must have reference to *The Rape of Lucrece*, a poem he had written a good many years before 1593. Here we have a deliberate deception and he waited a year to publish the already existing poem to complete the deception. The two dedications were potent devices used by Shake-speare to hide his true identity and to establish the fiction that he had commenced poet in 1593. Southampton had been used to verify that Shakspere was Shake-speare. So far as we know Southampton's verification was negative and not positive for history shows no other connection of Shake-speare-Southampton save the two dedications of which the second was couched in more intimate terms.

William of Stratford appeared in all his early legal records as Shakspere, Shagspere or Shaxpere. Now the change from Shakspere to Shakespeare is a small change and there is no reason why he should not have changed his name slightly if he wished to do so. Once altered, it would have been natural to leave it changed; nevertheless in his late life he signed his name over a period of years as William Shakspere or an abbreviated form of William Shakspere. The signature on the last page of the will can be deciphered as, "By me, William Shakspeare." The two formal dedications to Southampton were the only two times in which the author identified himself as William Shakespeare.

How very convenient to have two dedications and only two dedications to explain; how convenient for the purpose of disguise to have this double link between the poet and a single historical character and that at only one short period of time, 1593–94. How convenient that these two dedications came before any plays or any other works of Shake-speare had been published, so that future publishers would have a written record of who the author was and how he spelled his name. To judge from Southampton's role in history he had a charming personality but was none too bright. He attended plays with the Queen, he had some knowledge of the drama, and he had seen an actor on the stage with a name like Shake-speare. Southampton would have been surprised if some poet had not made dedications to him. The current genre of euphuism was disappearing from drama but remained secure for a long time in epistles and especially in dedications. Convention demanded dedications phrased in the most exaggerated style and in the most affectionate terms. Southampton voiced no objections to the first dedication as merely being honor due to one in his exalted position, and the second dedication could be given a more intimate tone with comparative safety. Even if Southampton had objected to the more personal touch in the second dedication, it would have been beneath his dignity to have made a public issue of the matter, especially as he had let the first dedication pass in silence. William Shakspere and Henry Wriothesly for all we know might have been almost complete strangers.

George Bernard Shaw opined that Shake-speare could "have become one of the ablest men of his times . . . ," and other authorities have voiced similar convictions. Shake-speare would have excelled in any endeavor he tried and merely the fact that William Shakspere was a minor actor and never a star is enough evidence alone to remove him from consideration as the dramatist Shake-speare. To unseat William Shakspere to one's own personal conviction is a simple task but to unseat William and at one and the same time to crown another to the satisfaction of the public is a colossal feat, principally because authority has turned its back and closed its eyes. Mark Twain in his book, "Is Shakespeare Dead?" has this to say, "I am aware that when even the brightest mind in our world has been trained up from childhood in a super-stition of any kind, it will never be possible for that mind, in its maturity, to examine sincerely, dispassionately and conscientiously any evidence or any circumstance which shall seem to cast a doubt upon the validity of that superstition." Mark Twain, writing in 1909, was of the opinion that William Shakspere would not "have to vacate his pedestal this side of the year 2209."

Had Herbert Lawrence back in 1769 been fortunate enough to have produced the correct identification of Shake-speare instead of coming up with merely a logical contender, no doubt his pronounce-ment would have been generally accepted and the whole matter laid to rest. Francis Bacon was a magnificent Jack-of-all-trades; Shake-speare was a magnificent Jack-of-all-trades; that alone made Bacon and Shake-speare cousins. Furthermore Bacon adhered to the Ptolemaic system, which regarded the earth as the central body of the universe (with its corollary order-disorder antithesis); like-wise Shake-speare adhered to the Ptolemaic system. But right here we start entertaining doubts about Bacon. Here we have a formal philosopher and a formal scientist (who appreciated the inductive method) who never accepted the Copernican theory even though Galileo proved the theory by the use of his invention, the telescope, in 1610 and published the theory at Rome in 1613 in his "Letters on the Solar Spots"; Bacon lived until 1626. Bacon had pedantic characteristics; he insisted on writing his works in Latin, his judg-ment was often faulty, and he lived in the past and by maxims of the past. Shake-speare had unerring judgment; he lived in the future with maxims of the present. Shake-speare was not a scien-tist, for if he had been a scientist he would have been a myriad-minded scientist and would have been intrigued and influenced by the Copernican theory even before it was proven by Galileo's ex-periments in astronomy.

The cousin relationship is not enough; Shake-speare and X need to be twins, twins in their ideas and their ideals; twins who fit into a logical time-scale; twins who are equally myriad-minded and equally high in the scale of NEGATIVE CAPABILITY. The Shake-speare scholarship since 1936 being more critical and more sci-entific should afford a new look on the possibility of such twinning.

Chapter VI

THE FOLIOS

Dedication Prefixed to the Folio of 1623
"To the most noble and incomparable pair of brethren,
William, Earl of Pembroke, etc., Lord Chamberlain to the King's
most excellent majesty, and
Philip, Earl of Montgomery, etc., Gentleman of his majesty's bed-
chamber,
Both Knights of the noble order of the Garter, and our singular
good lords."

The fresh Shake-speare scholarship of the past twenty years obligates a picture of the poet as a man sharply aware of the necessity for order, and also as a man motivated by a strong conviction that his duty was to instruct the present and future generations. It is unthinkable that Shake-speare should have been careless about the preservation of his manuscripts or thoughtless concerning either the publication of his Sonnet Folio or the publication of his Play Folio.

Shake-speare laid his plans with meticulous attention to detail. Not only were his manuscripts left with responsible people, but with responsible people who would be financially able to subsidize the printing of the folios of the sonnets and the plays. Such prerequisites were possessed by both the Southamptons and the Pembrokes. Historic data have indicated that Shake-speare's choice was the Pembrokes. The Pembrokes were a better literary choice, too, for the Dowager Countess of Pembroke had been a joint-author with her famous poet brother, Philip Sidney, and was also a poet and dramatist in her own right. Mary Pembroke would make a most excellent editor of the Play Folio and of the Sonnet Folio.

The essentials of the long dedication to the brothers are contained in these extracts, "But since your Lordships have been pleased to think these trifles something heretofore, and have prosecuted both them and their author living with so much favour, . . . For so much were your Lordship's likings of the several parts when

57

they were acted, as before they were published, the volume asked to be yours. We have but collected them, and done an office to the dead, to procure his orphans guardians; without ambition either of self-profit or fame; only to keep the memory of so worthy a friend and fellow alive as was our Shakespeare, by humble offer of his plays to your noble patronage . . ."

The dedication to the brothers Pembroke was signed by John Heminge and Henry Condell, fellow actors of William Shakspere. Along with Richard Burbage, Heminge and Condell and certain Stratford friends had received memento rings under the will of William in 1616. Burbage died in 1619 or his name no doubt would also have been used to help to prove again the fiction that William Shakspere was Shake-speare.

The Pembroke dedication and a second dedication, "To the great variety of readers," may have been written by Ben Jonson, who wrote one of the memorial poems for the First Folio; or by Edward Blount, the skilled writer among the publishers; or perhaps by Mary, Countess of Pembroke, for although she died in 1621, she was the logical "work-horse" of the Folio group for the years 1619, 1620, and 1621. According to Willoughby, the Folio went to press in 1621.

John Heminge and Henry Condell lacked the ability to compose such dedications. Heminge and Condell served a double purpose; they were the figureheads used to foster on the public the impression that actor and dramatist were one, and they also served as the representatives of the "King's Men." Early in 1619 William Jaggard and Thomas Pavier, who had limited copyrights to ten of Shake-speare's plays, several of which were bad-quarto editions, announced their intention to the Company of Stationers of printing this ten-play collection as "Works of William Shake-speare." William Pembroke as Lord Chamberlain was in a position to quash this undesirable project of Jaggard and Pavier and he did so in a letter dated May 3, 1619 in which he provided that none of the plays of the "King's Men" should be printed "without *some* of their consents." William Jaggard was drawn into the group in charge of publishing the First Folio. By 1621 he had become almost totally blind and had ceded his place to his son, Isaac.

Heminge and Condell did not give any details as to when, how, where, or from whom "We have but collected them" but they did furnish one vivid and important clue when they related to whoever composed the Folio dedications that, "and what he thought, he uttered with that easiness, that we have scarce received from him a blot in his papers." This implied that William Shakspere had seldom if ever been observed by his fellow actors to make any alterations in the manuscripts he brought to the theatre. The mechanics of the deception was probably as follows. Shake-speare presented a play to the Master of Revels for censorship when according to the master-plan he considered that it was time to have said play appear on the stage. The Master of Revels thereupon turned over to William Shakspere a copy of said play (but not in Shake-speare's handwriting). William Shakspere brought the play to the theatre but never blotted same.

From some source there appeared eighteen of Shake-speare's plays never before published to be added to the eighteen already published to make up the thirty-six plays of the First Folio. *Pericles*, the thirty-seventh play, was included in later folios. William Shakspere said not a word about any manuscripts in his elaborate and detailed will. Heminge and Condell gave no indication that they had received any manuscripts from William Shakspere. The "King's Men" were not mentioned as a source of the eighteen new plays; in fact the "King's Men" were not mentioned in the Folio at all. Of all the persons connected with the First Folio, the Pembrokes were the logical choice as the source of the eighteen new plays.

There were several pages of dedication and explanation prefacing the First Folio of plays. In contrast there were only thirty words of explanation about the First Sonnet Folio of 1609:

"To The Onlie Begetter Of
These Insuing Sonnets
Mr. W. H. All Happinesse
And That Eternitie
Promised
By
Our Ever-Living Poet
Wisheth
The Well-Wishing
Adventurer In
Setting
Forth
T. T."

The critics are in complete disagreement as to the meaning of these thirty words. T. T. stands for Thomas Thorpe, the publisher of the First Sonnet Folio: but the identity of T. T. is all that is known for certain. Those authorities who see the First Sonnet Folio as a pirated edition are anything but convincing in their arguments. That an obscure publisher like Thomas Thorpe might somehow pirate twenty or thirty sonnets is believable, since Francis Meres says they circulated among Shake-speare's private friends, but how can we reconcile the pirating of the mass of 154 sonnets? "Onlie Begetter" denotes *inspirer* to some; to others "Onlie Begetter" signifies the mere obtainer or procurer of the sonnets for Thorpe. Many different candidates have been put forward as Mr. W. H., the inspirer; none of them are satisfactory. Some say that the use of the phrase "Our Ever-Living Poet" is a lucid indication that the poet was dead by 1609; other critics think best to ignore this suggestion.

Because the dedication is a labyrinth of utter perplexity, we would have a sounder understanding of the body of the sonnets, if the thirty words had never been written. Since the result obtained by the Folio dedication was to make the interpretation of the sonnets more difficult, perhaps the dedication was carefully worded with the deliberate intent of creating such a state of confusion.

The first seventeen sonnets all urge the "lovely boy" to marry. E. K. Chambers says the "lovely boy" would have to be at least eighteen years of age at the time Sonnet 1 was written. There are no W. H.'s to fit such an age requirement. William Herbert, Earl of Pembroke, was born in 1580 and would have been only seven years of age in 1587. If somehow the initials were reversed by Thorpe, and Henry Wriothesly, Earl of Southampton, should become a candidate, we have the same difficulty. Southampton was only fourteen in 1587.

If "Onlie Begetter" simply means the mere obtainer or procurer of the sonnets for Thorpe, there are three likely candidates for Mr. W. H. Least likely is Henry Wriothesly, because there is no sensible reason for the reversal of the initials W. H. More plausible is the explanation for William Harvey, Southampton's father-in-law. The Dowager Countess of Southampton died in 1607, presumably leaving her personal effects at the disposal of her third husband, William Harvey. If these 154 sonnets happened to be in the possession of the Countess, and William Harvey happened to take them to Thomas Thorpe for publication, the publication date of 1609 would fit very well. If either the Southamptons or the Pembrokes had possession of the sonnet manuscripts in 1609, that fact would in itself argue that Shake-speare was dead by 1609. As has already been mentioned, "Our Ever-Living Poet" is the type of expression used to describe a dead poet. A third and the most forceful argument that the Sonnet Folio was posthumous is that Thomas Thorpe or Thomas Thorpe's backer had to write the dedication. If Shake-speare were alive in 1609, why did he not write his own dedication to the First Sonnet Folio?

The most reasonable choice for Mr. W. H. (as procurer, not inspirer) is William Herbert and either he or his mother, Mary, Countess of Pembroke, wrote the Sonnet dedication and edited the Sonnet Folio. William Herbert took the sonnets and the dedication to Thorpe with the request that Thorpe allow his initials, T. T., to be used at the bottom of the dedication; a request Thorpe would be more than willing to grant the Lord Chamberlain. William Herbert for a number of reasons fits Mr. W. H. better than either member of the Southampton family. The Pembrokes, with their literary advantages, were the best possible choice for the preservation of both the play manuscripts and the sonnet manuscripts. We know that they were connected with the Play Folio and this circumstance strengthens the notion that they were also connected with the Sonnet Folio. The "Will Sonnets" are deemed somewhat incongruous to the rest of the "dark lady" group of sonnets and several writers have visualized the "Will Sonnets" as compositions of some member of the Pembroke family. It is conceivable that the "Will Sonnets" might have been written by William Herbert or Mary Pembroke or Philip Sidney. "Will" could be either William Herbert or Philip Sidney, since Philip Sidney was known to his intimates as Willie and even appears in contemporary poetry as "pleasant Willie."

Consider carefully the intricate problems of the editor of the First Sonnet Folio if that editor happened to be Shake-speare's true friend and committed to sustain Shake-speare's mask. The sonnets must be published, for Shake-speare's reputation as a poet must be established by the masterful sonnets rather than the already published immature "ice-houses" of *Venus and Adonis* and *The Rape of Lucrece.* Yet the sonnets were extremely personal; they would be dynamite if the sonnet personalities could be translated into flesh and blood men and women. The editor compromised by concocting an ingenious piece of double talk for a dedication and carefully obscuring other landmarks, but still maintaining his (or her) integrity because none of the facts were actually misstated—the facts were only muddled.

The only division in the Sonnet Folio between the main body of the sonnets, 1–126, and the "dark lady" sonnets, 127–152, is a single black line between sonnet 126 and sonnet 127. The tone and texture of the "lovely boy" sonnets is so foreign to the tone and texture of the "dark lady" sonnets that the two sonnet divisions should have different titles. The "lovely boy" sonnets could be called "Sonnets to Light," "Sonnets to Love," "Sonnets to Beauty," "Sonnets to Order," or "Sonnets to Immortality." The "dark lady" sonnets might bear a title like "Sonnets to Darkness," "Sonnets to Hate," "Sonnets to Jealousy," "Sonnets to Disorder," or "Sonnets to Lust." The usual practice is for a writer to treat the subjects of lust and hate and jealousy as other people's lust and hate and jealousy. The "lovely boy" sonnets are personal, the "dark lady" twenty-six impersonal; Shake-speare is not one of the actors in the "dark lady" sonnets as he is in the first 126 sonnets.

Had the twenty-six "dark lady" sonnets been omitted altogether, Shake-speare's reputation as a poet would be even higher. What purpose did the "dark lady" sonnets serve? We do not have to ask why the "dark lady" sonnets had to be written in the first person because sonnets are first person singular vehicles. A sonnet does not lose its appeal because the poet is writing about two other people but pretends to be one of those two; "confession" is a potent and exciting medium. Shake-speare wrote the "dark lady" sonnets as a part of his disguise. The "Will Sonnets," whether composed by Shake-speare or by one of the Pembrokes, included as a part of the "dark lady" sonnets, expanded and enhanced the masquerade.

Nothing but confusion can arise from attempting to reconcile the personality of the "lovely boy" poet and the "dark lady" poet, yet the same author wrote both. The "lovely boy" sonnets as a whole give a true picture of Shake-speare; they are personal and they do reflect the personal emotions of the poet. The "dark lady" sonnets are not personal; Shake-speare is writing drama in a poetic form, he is detailing the volcanic emotional conflict between two individuals, neither to be identified with himself. The main body of the sonnets, 1–126, give a picture of Shake-speare; the "dark lady" sonnets, 127–152, do not. We will now explore the main body of the sonnets for character traits of Shake-speare.

Chapter VII

THE SONNETS

"I've reared a monument, my own,
More durable than brass,
Yea, kingly pyramids of stone
In height it doth surpass
Rain shall not sap, nor driving blast
Disturb its settled base,
Nor countless ages rolling past
Its symmetry deface.
I shall not wholly die, some part
Nor that a little, shall
Escape the dark destroyer's dart
And his grim festival."

Ode Epilogue of Horace

Shake-speare did not strive for originality in his sonnets any more than he did in his plays. In the dramas his style and the foreground of his thought derived from his fellow University Wits; his classic background was the broadest possible including derivations from Sophocles, Euripides, Aeschylus, Aristophanes, Darius Phrygius, Ovid, Horace, Virgil, Lucretius, Statius, Catullus, Seneca, Terence, and Plautus. The inspiration for his sonnets came principally from Ovid's *Metamorphosis*, various poetry of Horace, and from Chaucer's *Roman de la Rose*. As Francis Meres has indicated, Shake-speare as a poet was closer to Ovid than to any other writer. A comparison of Shake-speare's time sonnets with the *Epilogue to the Odes of Horace*, quoted above, will show the similarity of thought and expression between the two poets. Apparently, contemporary poets had relatively little influence on Shake-speare's sonnets, which argues that he was one of the first Elizabethans in the sonnet field. Since the sonnet fashion reached its peak in the 1590's, it is natural to assume that Shake-speare wrote his sonnets before the 1590's. Therefore, we have an independent indication that Mr. Hotson's date of composition for the sonnets is correct.

64

Many interpretations can be put upon the sonnets. Some critics view them as allegorical, some think that they are more dramatic than personal, others that they might have been written merely as exercises in the art of composition in the sonnet form. All of these various elements probably play a part. We will never know just how personal or just how artificial the sonnets are. Since the poet is of necessity a central figure in a sonnet as he is not in a play, the literary detective, while he knows he is on shaky ground because of the latitude allowed by poetic license, nevertheless is so starved for clues he is bound to speculate on the possible revelations as to the poet's character, physical attributes, and identity contained in the sonnets. The literary detective hopes that the sonnets are as personal as E. K. Chambers thinks they are by his, "Here are souls that pulse and words that burn."

The first 126 sonnets are written in admiration of the physical, mental, and spiritual beauty of a "lovely boy." The next twenty-six are principally devoted to condemning the infamous "dark lady" as a wanton with a soul as dark as her complexion. The narrative of the "lovely boy" and the narrative of the "dark lady" taken together strike a most discordant note. The sixteenth century was still the age of chivalry. The story of King Arthur and his Knights of the Round Table continued to be the most popular story in England. No small percentage of the populace took the story to be history and actually awaited King Arthur to return as he had promised. The Tudors claimed to be descended from Arthur through Owen Tudor, grandfather of Henry VII. Serious writers suggested that Queen Elizabeth was the embodiment of King Arthur and that the Elizabethan Age was the Golden Age of the return of Arthur. A poet was expected to sing the praises of some beautiful lady and by the same token, I suppose, a poetess would be expected to dwell on the admirable qualities of some beautiful boy or beautiful man. But here we have a poet singing a boy's praises and throwing mud on his lady. This is certainly a maladjustment. T. G. Tucker decries the lack of "decent taste and ordinary chivalry" in most of the "dark lady" sonnets.

In 1640 John Benson edited and published a medley of Shakespeare's sonnets in which in some cases he altered the sex of the addressee by switching the pronouns. Through the influence of Benson and others, the view was generally adopted that the main body of the sonnets was addressed to a woman. Samuel Coleridge took the position that the main body of the sonnets, "could only have come from a man deeply in love, and in love with a woman." For a century and a half, the presumption prevailed that the addressee was a woman; then came a reversal. Edmund Malone took up the study of changing the male pronouns to female pronouns and after extensive research arrived at the conclusion that the main body of the sonnets was addressed to a man. Edmund Malone established this hypothesis as the correct theory and his views have prevailed down to the present. Malone was a thorough and competent research worker on Shake-speare. He it was who discovered the poaching story of William Shakspere's youth had to be false because Sir Thomas Lucy did not have a deer park until much later. Malone also exposed a number of Shakespearean forgeries.

Somewhere or somehow there appears to be a *misplaced gender* about the sonnets. Barrett Wendell recoiled at the idea of myriad-minded Shake-speare sincerely prostrating himself before a boy patron; then reminded himself of Elizabeth Barrett Browning's *Sonnets from the Portuguese*; she was six years older than her "lovely boy," Robert Browning.

The picture of the "lovely boy" as generated by expressions in the sonnets is very flattering. He is "the world's fine ornament," a "beauteous and lovely youth." He is in his late teens or early twenties, "And thou presents't a pure, unstained prime." He has red or auburn hair, "And buds of marjoram had stol'n thy hair." The boy is as fair in disposition and mental ability as he is fair of face, "Fair, kind and true, is all my argument"; also "Thou art as fair in knowledge as in hue." The beautiful youth has a beautiful mother and we have a hint that Shake-speare has known her in her lovely girlhood:

> "Thou art thy mothers' glass, and she in thee
> Calls back the lovely April of her prime";

What is meant by the seventh line of Sonnet 20: "A man in hue all hues in his controlling"? Gerald Massey suggests that it might refer to Robert Devereux, Earl of Essex, who had for one of his titles, *Ewe.* Herman Conrad for a number of reasons selected the Earl of Essex as the "lovely boy." In the Encylopedia Britannica, E. K. Chambers mentions this choice of Essex, disagrees with the idea, but praises Conrad's work in general. Essex had auburn hair. He was born on November 19, 1566 and would have been twenty in April 1587, which would fit the time requirements perfectly.

We see personal allusions to Shake-speare in some ten sonnets.

Sonnet 22

"My glass shall not persuade me I am old,
So long as youth and thou are of one date;
But when in thee time's furrows I behold,
Then look I death my days should expiate."

Sonnet 37

"So I, made lame by fortune's dearest spite
Take all my comfort of thy worth and truth;"

Sonnet 48

"But thou, to whom my jewels trifles are,"

and

"Within the gentle closure of my breast,"

Sonnet 62

"But when my glass shows me myself indeed,
Bated and chopp'd with tann'd antiquity"

and

"Painting my age with beauty of thy days"

Sonnet 63

"Against my love shall be, as I am now
With Time's injurious hand crush'd and
        o'erworn;"

Sonnet 72

"My name be buried where my body is"

Sonnet 73

"That time of year thou may'st in me behold
When yellow leaves, or none, or few, do hang
Upon those boughs which shake against the cold,
Bare ruin'd choirs, where late the sweet
        birds sang.

In me thou see'st the twilight of such day
As after sunset fadeth in the west;"

Sonnet 76

"Why write I still all one, ever the same,
And keep invention in a noted weed,
That every word doth almost tell my name,
Showing their birth and where they did
      proceed?"

Sonnet 89

"Speak of my lameness, and I straight will
      halt,"

Sonnet 94

"They that have power to hurt and will do
      none,
That do not do the thing they most do show,
Who, moving others are themselves as stone,
Unmoved, cold, and to temptation slow;
They rightly do inherit heaven's graces,
And husband nature's riches from expense;"

The ideas expressed by Sonnets 72, 76, and 94 might be guide-posts and then again, they might not be. *Perhaps* Sonnets 72 and 76 are hints as to Shake-speare's identity. *Perhap*s Sonnet 94 is autobiographical. From Sonnets 37 and 89 we gain the impression that Shake-speare is lame or has been lame some time in the past. There should be no doubt that the four age sonnets, 22, 62, 63, and 73 mean what they say in the absence of any contradictory evidence in the rest of the sonnets. Another age sonnet, number 138, has not been quoted because it is a member of the "dark lady" sonnets in which we believe Shake-speare is speaking with another's voice and gazing with another's eyes. The age sonnets plainly relate that in 1587 Shake-speare was middle-aged, perhaps forty or fifty. In this year, William Shakspere was in his early twenties.

Gerald Massey was of the opinion that Sonnet 48 was spoken by a man to a woman, but J. M. Robertson comments of Massey, "he instantly evokes the rejoinder that it is more fitly to be conceived as addressed by a woman to a man." The only solution that will completely lay to rest the problem of the *misplaced gender* of the main body of the sonnets is to assume that *Shake-speare* was a woman. A fantastic idea? Hardly, when for years Mary, Countess of Pembroke, has been seriously considered as a candidate for Shake-speare's position. T. W. Baldwin is of the opinion that both the "dark lady" sonnets of the 127–152 series and the allusion to a lady in Sonnets 40, 41, and 42 are purely literary fictional fabrications. If such be the proper interpretation, then for the sonnets to have been written by a woman makes even greater sense. It would be quite natural for a woman to feel called upon to show her esteem and admiration for a lovely boy.

In the two books of Frank Harris, *The Man Shakespeare* and *The Women of Shakespeare*, the author many times points out the womanly qualities of Shake-speare. In the introduction to *The Women of Shakespeare* he makes this explanation about choosing a title for the book: "Here again Shakespeare will reveal himself as the gentle, irresolute, meditative poet-thinker-lover we learned to know in the Orsino-Hamlet-Antony, an aristocrat of most delicate sensibilities and sympathetic humour whose chief defects are snobbishness and overpowering sensuality, if indeed this latter quality is not to be reckoned a virtue in an artist or at least an endowment. But the public probably would have misunderstood the title *The Woman Shakespeare*, and so I changed it to *The Women of Shakespeare*." Mary Fitton has long been the popular choice for the dubious honor of being the "dark lady" of the sonnets. Mary Fitton was Frank Harris' enthusiastic choice. Toward the end of the book *The Women of Shakespeare*, Harris says: "Mary Fitton was so strong that she seems to have been the positive or masculine element and Shakespeare so gentle-sensitive that he was the feminine element in the strange union. The soul has not always the sex of the body." We agree with but little of what Mr. Harris has to say. For entirely different reasons we can see feminine traits in Shake-speare.

Does Mary Herbert, Countess of Pembroke, fit the time-scale? She does not. In April 1587 she was twenty-five and would hardly fit either the age or the time sonnets. Furthermore, she would be about the last person in the world to have had a love affair with the Earl of Essex or anyone else. Only the year before, her beloved brother had been killed in The Netherlands in battle; Mary was busy with her husband and her young children; apparently she was content and happy except for the shadow of the death of Philip Sidney.

We have another woman candidate; she fits the age sonnets perfectly, and in April 1587 she fell in love with Robert Devereux, Earl of Essex. On May 3, 1587, one Anthony Bagot wrote a letter in which he said, "When she is abroad, nobody with her but my lord of Essex, and at night my lord is at cards, or one game or another with her, that he cometh not to his own lodging till birds sing in the morning." The lady was none other than England's queen, Elizabeth Tudor. She was fifty-three, her lovely boy but twenty; a much greater discrepancy than between Elizabeth Barrett Browning and Robert Browning. Elizabeth Tudor was charming at any age and she was a great and noble queen.

The critics specify that Sonnet 104 was written for a birthday or some other kind of an anniversary. We have already learned from Leslie Hotson that Sonnets 104, 107, 123, and 124 were composed late in the year 1589. The birthday of Essex was on November 19; cold weather had no doubt set in by November 19, 1589, which would have fulfilled all the requirements of Sonnet 104 and would place the composition of Sonnet 1 in April 1587. The expressions in Sonnet 104 "Since first your eye I eyed" and "Since first I saw you fresh" mean *since the day I discovered my love for you*. Elizabeth had known Essex as a child, but April 1587 was the first time she had met the man Essex, the warrior returning from the Lowlands campaign.

Elizabeth and Essex were parted on several occasions during the three-year interval 1587–89. Sonnets 26–32, Sonnets 43–52, Sonnets 56–61, and Sonnets 97–99 were written during periods of absence. Late in the year 1590, the Earl of Essex secretly married the widow of Sir Philip Sidney. When Queen Elizabeth found out about the marriage she was exceedingly angry, but was somewhat mollified when Essex consented that his wife should live "very retired in her mother's house." E. K. Chambers suggested that Shake-speare wrote *Romeo and Juliet* because of a perturbing love experience through which he had just passed. From the London earthquake reference we can fix the date of the composition of *Romeo and Juliet* as 1591, the next year after Essex's marriage.

The reference to Shake-speare's lameness in Sonnets 37 and 89 may be explained as meaning the sore on Elizabeth's leg that bothered her for a number of years. On July 1, 1570, De Spes, the Spanish Ambassador, in a letter to Madrid reported that "The illness of the Queen is caused by an open ulcer above the ankle, which prevents her from walking." Sonnet 37, however, may refer to a more lamentable lameness. Ben Jonson's story to a tavern friend that the Queen ". . . had a membrana on her, which made her uncapable of man, . . ." finds a striking parallel in Sonnet 37, which strongly suggests sexual lameness.

"So I, made lame by fortune's dearest spite,
Take all my comfort of thy worth and truth."

Lytton Strachey in his *Elizabeth and Essex* informed the public that Elizabeth and Essex contended "like school children" in the realm of learning and literature. The sonnets were Elizabeth's part of that contention, which was echoed centuries later when another poetess wrote *Sonnets from the Portuguese* to her younger love, Robert Browning. The writer of the sonnets was also the writer of the thirty-seven plays and the two long poems. There is too much parallelism of thought, word, and style between the sonnets, *Venus and Adonis, The Rape of Lucrece, Love's Labour's Lost, The Comedy of Errors, The Two Gentlemen of Verona, Romeo and Juliet, King Henry VI, A Midsummer Night's Dream, King John,* and other plays for there to be any doubt on this point.

Somerset Maugham points out that involved expressions in letter writing do not predicate involved play composition: ". . . English prose is elaborate rather than simple. It was not always so. Nothing could be more racy, straightforward and alive than the prose of Shakespeare; but it must be remembered that this was dialogue written to be spoken. We do not know how he would have written if like Corneille he had composed prefaces to his plays. It may be that they would have been as euphuistic as the letters of Queen Elizabeth."

When would a busy queen have time to write plays? We might well ask: When would a busy actor, memorizing play after play, have time to write? It is a well-known maxim that you go to a busy person to get things done. The very fact that there are

no plays with Elizabeth as authoress creates the suspicion there
must be hidden plays of hers. A born competitor, she was bound
to experiment with every type of writing, and she surely would
not completely neglect the most popular narrative medium of her
age, namely, the drama. She was keenly interested in the development of the play medium from the moralities through the blank
verse of *Gorbuduc* and up through the finished product of the
University Wits. She witnessed the beginnings and gradual development of the drama: she probably saw more plays than any person
in her time. She fought the Puritans to keep open the theatres.
Elizabeth liked what the people liked and what Shake-speare liked.
John Middleton Murry explains how she made possible Elizabethan drama:

> "In so far as Shakespeare had to please the Court—
> which he had to do—it resolved into pleasing the Queen.
> Not because of the money-reward earned by Court per-
> formances, but because the very existence of the players
> directly depended upon the royal authority. It was the
> royal countenance which enabled them to establish them-
> selves in the outskirts of London in spite of the bitter op-
> position of the puritan authorities of the City. The Queen
> liked to be amused, but she did not like to pay for her
> amusement. It was a blessed conjuncture for the Eliza-
> bethan drama. The Privy Council issued warrants to the
> players during the plague on the ground that 'they may be
> in the better readiness hereafter for her Majesty's service
> whensoever they shall be thereupon called.'
>
> "To please the people, to please the Queen, and to
> please himself—these were the driving motives of the
> period of Shakespeare's career which culminated in *Ham-
> let*. And he was the kind of man to be able to do all at
> once: and the Queen was the kind of Queen to make it
> easy for him, because she had fundamentally the same
> tastes as the people. She liked the plays they liked; and
> they liked the plays she liked—at bottom."

We see in Shake-speare Elizabeth's twin. Their myriad in-
tellects neither clashed nor diverged; they always saw eye to eye.
The political propaganda in the plays never came in for any act

of censorship because it was written exactly as Elizabeth would write it. Their philosophy was the same, their religion was the same, their intense patriotic devotion to England was the same, their desire to instruct while amusing was the same. Tucker Brooke writes of Elizabeth: "With whom are we to match her? With whom but with the man of Stratford, the greatest of all her subjects, her mightiest colleague in building the age we know alternately by both their names? . . . And at the end there are no better words to apply to Elizabeth than those Arnold addressed to her poet:

> " 'Others abide our question. Thou art free.
> We ask and ask: Thou smilest and art still,
> Out-topping knowledge.' "

J. E. Neale writes, "Elizabeth had no intention of surrendering her powers, or acquiescing in men's views of women. She had a great longing, she said, 'to do some act that would make her fame spread abroad in her lifetime, and, after, occasion memorial for ever.' " We are on firm ground when we assume that Elizabeth, in choosing a pen name, would use her fine intelligence to formulate a nom de plume that would be appropriate and fitting, yet would be ingenious enough to preserve her secret at least until well after her death. It is very much like that thoughtful queen to do as thorough a job as possible in inventing a foolproof disguise for her authorship.

Elizabeth Tudor would no doubt have been pleased to have been able to follow the advice of Theodore Roosevelt to "talk softly and carry a big stick," if she had been possessed of a big stick. The English of her day as well as the English of today were opposed to a large standing army. Her navy against the Spanish Armada was only a handful of small vessels. She was banking on the skill of her naval architects and the superior abilities of her great sea captains to carry off the victory. Elizabeth ruled half a small island with a total English population of about four million. Little wonder she found the only practical political policy was to "talk a good fight and run scared." When Spain got tough she became chummy with France, and when France became quarrelsome she made overtures to Philip. All English sovereigns were perpetually in need of money. Elizabeth was no exception. She encouraged Sir Francis Drake to seize Spain's homeward-bound gold ships and then informed Philip that she simply could not control her pirate merchantmen. The great Queen understood full well the futility of battle (exactly the same lesson explained by Shake-speare in *Troilus and Cressida*) and she would not go to war if there was any way to avoid the conflict. Elizabethan England would not have been a world power had it not been for the adroitness with which Elizabeth maintained the balance of power in Europe, and she did it by shaking-a-speare—that is to say, she knew how to make a show of strength where a show of strength was needed and to keep one and all, even her Privy Council, in doubt as to her next political move. The pen name Shake-speare had to be appropriate; it was. Shake-speare had to be subtle; it was, as the passage of time well testified. Shake-speare had to appear in the image of a flesh-and-blood man of a similar name; this was arranged. Shake-speare had to appear in the image of a man, not a woman, because sixteenth century England would never forgive a woman, let alone a queen, for writing down-to-earth realism, and that was the way Elizabeth wanted to write. In order to test the good and bad qualities of a play, the author must obtain a completely frank expression of public opinion, which would only be frank if the literary effort were written anonymously or under a pen name, if said author is some great personage. Even in the nineteenth century, male prejudice being what it is, Mary Ann Evans Cross thought best to write as George Eliot; and Charlotte, Emily, and Anne Bronte as Currer Bell, Ellis Bell, and Acton Bell.

Brakspeare and Hurlspeare are warlike names without a doubt. Shake-speare has been called a warlike name, but when we stop to analyze the verb-noun combination, Shake-speare is more appropriately the name of a statesman, a politician, a sovereign, and a writer. Elizabeth was, in the highest sense, all four. To shake-a-speare, or to shake-the-speare, is in some instances a show of strength, sometimes it is a threat; in a broader sense it is a means of keeping the other fellow guessing as to just what your intentions are. It is a means of keeping your opponent or opponents wondering just how much strength you possess and just how you will employ said strength. To shake a weapon is to write—or should we say that to write is to shake a weapon and that a powerful writer wields a powerful weapon. The original sceptre may have been a speare; at least a sceptre and a speare are similar shafts. In a speech before the House of Commons in 1586, Elizabeth had this to say: "... Then to the end I might make the better progress in the art of *swaying the sceptre* I entered into long and serious cogitation what things were worthy and fitting for kings to do; and I found it was most necessary that they should be abundantly furnished with those special virtues, justice, temperance, prudence, and magnanimity,..."

Chapter VIII

NEGATIVE CAPABILITY

". . . several things dovetailed in my mind, and at once struck me what quality went to form a man of achievement, especially in literature, and which Shakespear possessed so enormously — I mean NEGATIVE CAPABILITY, *that is, when a man is capable of being in uncertainties, mysteries, doubts, without any irritable reaching after fact and reason."*

John Keats

We have observed some of the ways in which Shake-speare and Elizabeth were twins. In the realm of Negative Capability Shake-speare and Elizabeth were so much alike as to suggest identical twins. If Shake-speare was Master of the Philosophy of Negative Capability, Elizabeth was Doctor of the Philosophy of Negative Capability. We ordinary mortals strive for certainty and security; we like to solve a problem, put it behind us and go on to the next problem. Myriad-minded Shake-speare and myriad-minded Elizabeth knew that there is no human certainty nor human security, and that complex problems cannot be willfully solved; such problems must in part solve themselves with the aid of time. Patience, infinite patience, is all-important.

Of the many instances, large and small, in which Elizabeth demonstrated Negative Capability, we will consider only three: the marriage problem, the problem of Mary, Queen of Scots, and the succession problem. Actually the three problems blended together, for had Elizabeth thought it wise to marry and have children, the succession problem and the problem of Mary, Queen of Scots, would have been largely resolved.

Katherine Anthony makes the statement, "Elizabeth remains to this day one of the mysteries of history." She could not be called a womanly woman; she was too masculine. Her sexual and emotional disposition is a great enigma, and the reason for the enigma is that she combined the qualities of both sexes. She spat and swore like a man. Anthony says, "Some modern authorities have asserted that Elizabeth had no sexual impulse at all. . . . Her jokes were freer than was customary for her sex in those days and she competed, one assumes, very favorably with men." Katherine Anthony relates that the circumstances of her death defied custom: "At three o'clock in the morning of March 24, 1603, her body was pronounced to be lifeless. It was prepared for burial by her ladies and was not dissected and embalmed as was the rigorous custom in those days for sovereigns. No man's hand touched the body of Elizabeth; she probably had forbidden it. She went to her grave with her secret inviolate."

Modern psychology suggests that if any of Elizabeth's physicians ever told her she was incapable of bearing children, that verdict would have been enough to make her a lifelong spinster. Elizabeth was not being factitious when she remarked to Lord Sussex, "I hate the idea of marriage for reasons that I would not divulge to a twin soul."

Elizabeth had had many marriage proposals as a Princess; they were to multiply in number and expand in geography when she came to the throne. Her brother-in-law was her first serious suitor after she became queen. They bandied the idea back and forth between them. The Spanish Ambassador was all in favor of Philip coming to England with his army, marrying the new Queen, and lining up England as a Spanish possession. Elizabeth played for time, and Philip vacillated as he was wont to do. For long years Philip and Elizabeth went on playing a cat-and-mouse game, and ever the slow-to-act and slow-to-think Spanish monarch was cast in the role of the mouse. By the time Philip got around to making a definite offer of marriage, Elizabeth felt strong enough to repel any attempted invasion of the realm. She acknowledged the marriage offer in terms of unmeasured gratitude and affection, but could not bring herself to accept, not for a while at least. Marriage was a serious step, and she needed time to think it over. She could only promise that if she took a husband her brother-in-law would be preferred over all. If Good Queen Bess never accepted a proposal, she at least had the good grace never to refuse one; it was always maybe. "It was a form that, with the name left blank, she might have printed for future use!"

Elizabeth's ideal of a husband was a handsome, tolerant, kind, highly intelligent warrior-prince. History does not produce many princes in that mold and there were none around Europe in her day. Henry VIII as a youth, then only a second son, had been such a beau ideal. First English Prince with a Renaissance education, he was handsome, a star athlete, kindly, devout, an interesting talker, a fierce and courageous foe in battle; fortunate in all things but marriage. Elizabeth measured the institution of matrimony in the tragedy of her mother's marriage, in the frustration of her father's marriages, and in the debit of English blood and English treasure which had been her half-sister Mary's Spanish marriage. She measured each and every one of her long line of suitors by the yardstick of her father as a young man, and none of them came close to standing tall enough. Edward Courtney, the Earl of Arundel, Prince Philip, Sir William Pickering, Henry Stuart Darnley, Archduke Ferdinand, Duke Adolphus of Denmark, Prince Eric of Sweden, Archduke Charles, Duke Hans Casimer, King Charles IX of France, Prince Don John, the Duke of Anjou, and the Duke of Alencon were all tested and found wanting. One was too old, a few were too young, one was an imbecile, several were bigoted and intolerant, one had pockmarks, and most of them were dull. But what of Robert Dudley, the Queen's favorite of favorites? The Earl of Leicester was handsome, courageous, and charming. An observation by Katherine Anthony may indicate why even Dudley did not measure up to marriage specifications: "The generation of Lord Leicester was the last which dared present itself at court without a university diploma. The favorites who came after him were all lettered men, the fruit of the educational foundations . . . The queen bandied verses with them and flirted by means of riddles and epigrams."

Arthur D. Innes saw clearly the Negative Capability of Elizabeth in her marriage ventures: "She had played the farce for years with Archduke Charles; she had played it with Henry of Anjou; she had already played it with Alencon once; yet every time she started it afresh, potentates and ambassadors, her own ministers, and the wooer she selected, took the thing seriously, played into her hands, and were cajoled by her boundless histronic ingenuity. Either she treated the world to a series of successful impositions, carried through unaided and unsuspected with the supreme audacity and skill of a consummate comedienne; or she was a contemptibly capricious woman whose inordinate vacillations invariably took the turn which after-events proved to have been the luckiest possible in the circumstances. Of these two interpretations, the theory of the deliberate policy is the more acceptable, if only because it is inconceivable that the habitual indulgence of sheer wanton caprice should never once have involved her in some irrevocable blunder, some position from which she could not be extricated. Yet history affords no parallel to such a repeatedly and universally successful dissimulation."

Along the line of general policy Innes saw her methods as ingenious and as devious as in her marriage transactions: "She drove Burghley and Walsingham almost to despair by her caprices; but if she overrode their judgment, it was not to displace them for other advisors more congenial to her mood, but to take affairs into her own hands and manipulate them with a cool defiance of apparent probabilities, a duplicity so audacious that it passed for a kind of sincerity, which gave her successes the appearance of being due to an almost supernatural good luck. Histrionics were her stock-in-trade: she was eternally playing a part, and playing it with such zest that she habitually cheated her neighbors, and occasionally even herself, into forgetting her role was merely assumed for ulterior purposes. When a crisis was reached where there was no further use for play-acting, she was again the shrewd practical ruler who had merely been masked as a comedienne. . . . But voracious as she was of flattery it never mislead her; behind the screen of capriciousness, an intellect was ever at work as cool and calculating as her grandfather's, as hard and resolute as her father's. To understand her people was her first aim; to make them great was her ultimate ambition. And she achieved both."

The World Book Encyclopedia says of Elizabeth, "Her reign became known as one of the most glorious periods in the history of her country. In her own time she was considered almost more than human, . . ." The Tudor myth together with the King Arthur-lives-again-in-Elizabeth myth were enough to make the sixteenth century view Elizabeth as supernatural. Maxwell Anderson, the American playwright, develops the Queen as having superhuman cunning in his two plays *Elizabeth the Queen* (1932) and *Mary of Scotland* (1933). The latter play is especially instructive in giving an insight into Elizabeth's character. Yet Elizabeth's handling of the Mary Queen of Scots problem was not so much cunning, superhuman or otherwise, as it was an adroit example of the force of Negative Capability. Elizabeth could not have foreseen all the consequences of the Darnley marriage as Maxwell Anderson implies; the Tudor moves and countermoves on the chessboard of political expediency as each new Scottish episode developed were Elizabeth's usual masterpieces of strategy.

In 1560, Mary Stuart was not only Queen and lawful ruler of Scotland but she was also Queen of France and next heir to the throne of England. She actually used the crests of English royalty on her tableware in France and asserted that she had a better claim to the English throne than Elizabeth, a claim that had some merit. On December 5th of that year her husband, Francis 2nd, King of France, died. Mary, a very young widow, was sure to marry again. When Mary returned to Scotland to rule that country, Elizabeth picked out a husband for Mary and proceeded to promote the marriage to a successful conclusion. Here is how it was done. Elizabeth said she wanted to see Mary with a proper husband and suggested that she send Robert Dudley to Scotland as a prospective suitor. Elizabeth promised to advance Robert to all possible honors if Mary would consent to the marriage, and she would favor Mary's title to the succession to the English throne in every way possible. Mary was hurt and angry at the suggestion that she should consent to marry Elizabeth's boy friend whom Elizabeth would not marry. Mary was more kindly disposed than ever to cast her lot with the tall, handsome Henry Stuart Darnley, who had come to Edinburgh early in 1565. Darnley, with the death of Edward Courtney, was the first male heir to the English throne; he was a great-grandson of Henry VII. Mary felt sure Elizabeth wanted her to marry Dudley and did not want her to marry Darnley—so she married Darnley. Darnley had been Elizabeth's candidate all the time. When a son was born to Mary and Darnley, Elizabeth pretended to receive the news as a blow; she bemoaned the fact that Mary could have a fine son, while she, Elizabeth, had none. The son of Mary and Darnley had an excellent claim on both the Scottish and the English thrones, and through this baby Elizabeth planned to unite England and Scotland forevermore; not a divided island but a united island. History played into Elizabeth's hands even more than she could have anticipated. Darnley, a weak and intemperate youth, soon revealed his true self to Mary. Mary's romantic love quickly cooled off. Darnley helped plan the murder of one of Mary's secretaries, David Riccio. For this and other unsavory acts on the part of Darnley, Mary lured her husband into a murder trap where Darnley lost his life. Mary then ran away and married James Bothwell, one of the ringleaders in the Darnley murder plot. The Scottish nobles were incensed, captured Mary, put her in prison, and made her abdicate as Queen and consent to have her year-old son become James VI of Scotland.

William Cecil, Lord Burghley, was an able and farsighted Secretary of State. When Cecil and Elizabeth disagreed as to policy, time would usually prove Cecil to be in the wrong, and such was the case in their divergent attitude toward the Queen of Scots. Cecil, like most of the world, recoiled at Mary's utter folly in being implicated in Darnley's murder. Mary had the scene rigged so that Bothwell "kidnaped" her and "forced" her into marriage, but she was too willing a victim for this subterfuge to fool anyone. Cecil pleaded with Elizabeth to wash her hands of the whole affair. Elizabeth as usual was thinking of the future of England, not just the local and immediate drama. She backed up her cousin Mary, demanded to know of the Scottish nobles how they dared to imprison their anointed Queen, and offered to act as an impartial judge in investigating the whole sordid affair. Mary took heart and started to plan her escape. She had many powerful friends who would sooner or later set her free. Had Elizabeth turned her back on Mary, Mary might have either summoned aid from France or escaped and fled to France. Mary in the hands of France would have been an active and intolerable pawn against the English throne. When Mary escaped she escaped to her "friend" England, and Elizabeth promptly put her trouble-making cousin into bondage for the rest of her life. Mary lived a genteel and courtly life as an English prisoner; she was allowed practically every privilege but escape. Plot against England she did many times; plot for the assassination of Elizabeth she did many times. At first Mary's mail was not restricted, but in time, after a few of Mary's intrigues had been uncovered, it was arranged so that Sir Francis Walsingham, the head of the English secret service, read all her outgoing and incoming mail. It was a letter from Mary, in her own handwriting, urging an assassin to murder Elizabeth, that led to her own execution, but that was not until early 1587.

Elizabeth's whole life was drama. She watched drama; she acted drama; she wrote drama, and she lived drama. E. C. Wilson told how she conquered the stage: "Her invincible wit that mastered any scene where mere male sense strutted, her personal courage that matched any man's, her force, energy and self-confidence drew Renaissance admiration of the masculine virtues even while her feminine charms aroused chivalric adoration of the lady. . . . She was the last of the Tudor dynasts, and she accepted her role in the worldly drama of power just as circumstances wrote it and with a readiness to use any tricks in the mundane play." Milton Waldman wrote along much the same lines: "She knew men far better than any man knew—or ever will know—her. Some she loved, some she trusted, but they were not the same . . . and a profound knowledge of how far a woman may safely trade on the inexhaustible vanity and ambition of men. . . . But she loathed war, then as always, with a statesman's distrust of its uncertainty and a woman's hatred of its bloodshed and expense. . . . She could always find time to interview distinguished foreigners or the young students whose education in foreign universities would be paid out of her own pockets, and to circulate amongst the great and the humble of her subjects."

Throughout her long reign the Queen sidestepped the naming of her successor. She stated her own life was less endangered and the life of her successor was safer to leave the issue suspended. Here again we meet Negative Capability. Apparently she favored James VI of Scotland, but it was not until she was so near death as to have lost her power of speech that she indicated by a motion that James was to have the throne when vacant.

In act 2, scene 1, of *A Midsummer Night's Dream*, Oberon speaks of Elizabeth:

> "And the imperial votaress passed on,
> In maiden meditation, fancy-free."

The "Imperial Votaress" made her three vows at the age of fifteen, at the age of twenty-five, and at the age of forty-five.

Elizabeth had reason to believe the interval of ten years and the interval of twenty years to be significant in her life pattern.

At fifteen the Seymour affair brought Elizabeth close to the brink of personal disaster and cost the Lord Admiral, Thomas Seymour, his head. Her first romance thus tragically put to an end, Elizabeth made a vow to celibacy. Never again would she allow her emotions to sway her mind. Marriage was a proven pitfall. The mind must rule the heart.

At twenty-five she became Queen and vowed that only England would be her husband. She placed a gold ring on her finger in token of her marriage to England and wore it all her life.

At forty-five she discovered that her favorite of favorites, Robert Dudley, had been married to her cousin Lettice Knollys for nearly a year. Elizabeth felt cheated; her anger, disgust, and loathing knew no bounds. As in other times of personal stress, she turned to reading and translation of the classics for relief. She found the character of Timon of Athens in either Lucian or Plutarch and proceeded to pour out her anger, disgust, and loathing in an oration against ingratitude in the form of a five-act play.

At forty-five she made a vow to literature. The children of her marriage to England would have to be literary children; she would leave her political acumen, economic wisdom, social philosophy, and religious convictions to future generations of Englishmen; "occasion memorial forever." The marriage farce was in its last chapter, the menopause either beginning or imminent; her memorial would have to be in words.

History does not record either the vow to celibacy at fifteen or the vow to literature at forty-five, yet the thoughtful historian will recognize the plausibility of both vows. Marriage meant an alliance. France feared such an alliance with Spain or Austria, and Spain feared a marriage alliance with France. Elizabeth played the marriage game for all it was worth, first with one and then the other of the rivals France and Spain. Her vow to celibacy was a completely hidden, private vow. To public view she had to appear as the most eligible of maidens and the most anxious to marry if only the right man would come along.

Likewise Elizabeth's vow to literature was a completely hidden, private vow, which must remain concealed to insure realistic writing and sincere criticism. Her authorship must also remain hidden because the world's opinion would be that in devoting so much time to literary effort she was neglecting her duties as sovereign.

Without even considering the time-scale, Elizabeth must be placed far ahead of the other candidates on the scale of probability. More than any other Elizabethan, the English Queen was the most likely to possess the 15,000-word vocabulary (estimated by one author to be 21,000 words). She was head and shoulders above her contemporaries in the art of Negative Capability; the perfect mistress of holding issues in suspension. She was a better linguist than any of the other candidates.

As a rule, Elizabeth consulted her councilors individually and then made up her mind what to do. The Queen, not the Privy Council, made foreign policy. No foreign ambassador spoke English; it was not the language of diplomacy. Yet Elizabeth was such a fine linguist she could deal directly with most ambassadors in their own tongue and she preferred to deal directly. The Queen maintained a large staff of secretaries, each one with his specialty. Usually these secretaries did the actual writing as she dictated. J. E. Neale said, "She had a real genius for this work, and no sovereign of her day maintained so close a monopoly on it." Thomas Windebank was made Clerk of the Signet in 1568 and Clerk of the Privy Seal in 1598. A most trusted aide, he was also Elizabeth's literary secretary. The line of Sonnet 72 "My name be buried where my body is" might signify that there were Shake-speare manuscripts ordered placed in the tomb of Elizabeth. Elizabeth's manuscripts would probably be in the handwriting of Sir Thomas Windebank.

Elizabeth had a better opportunity than any of the other candidates to know "thousands of people intimately" and to talk with and study "every class and condition of mankind and every class and condition of womankind." It is doubtful if anyone but a woman could understand women the way Shake-speare understood them.

Elizabeth became an authority on the seven seas from her talks with Drake, Howard, Raleigh, and other seafaring men. She knew the other countries of Europe minutely through her intimacy with foreign ambassadors, English ambassadors, marriage ambassadors, travelers, and the English students maintained in foreign universities through her generosity. She learned practical law from her councilors and magistrates. Elizabeth became an authority on war and military tactics by close association with her generals. Her position as an astute queen deepened and matured her "myriad-minded" capacity.

The next two chapters will relate the how, why, when, and where of the royal masquerade. To keep the narrative simple, the theory that Elizabeth and Shake-speare are one and the same will be presented as a fact.

Chapter IX

IMITATION OF THE GREEK

"I have a tree grows here in my close,
That mine own use invites me to cut down,
And shortly must I fell it; tell my friends,
Tell Athens, in the sequence of degree,
From high to low throughout, that who so please
To stop affliction, let him take his haste,
Come hither, ere my tree hath felt the axe,
And hang himself. I pray you, do my greeting."

Timon of Athens

Since English drama was destined to reach an all-time high in the 1580's and 1590's, the events of the late 1570's were a prelude to the golden days to come. In 1576 The Theatre was built and in the same year plays were first presented in a room of the dismantled Blackfriars. In 1577 The Curtain was built. Also in 1577 appeared the first edition of Holinshed's *Chronicles of England, Scotland and Ireland.* Holinshed was the chief source of Shake-speare's *Cymbeline, Lear,* and *Macbeth* as well as the ten history plays. In 1578 George Whetstone published *Promos and Cassandra,* the source of Shake-speare's *Measure for Measure.* In September of 1578, Robert Dudley, Earl of Leicester, the Queen's favorite of favorites, secretly married the Dowager Countess of Essex, Lettice Knollys. When the secret became known to Elizabeth, the world would rock.

1579

On April 6, 1580 London was shaken by a severe earthquake. This quake was felt throughout all of England. Exactly one year prior to the earthquake, April 6, 1579, Sir Thomas North entered his *Plutark's Lyves* in the Stationers' Register. He paid his license fee and deposited a copy of his manuscript ('XV^s and a copie'). North's English translation of *Plutarch's Lives* was the working source of *Timon of Athens* as it was for the three Roman plays of Shake-speare, *Coriolanus, Julius Caesar,* and *Antony and Cleopatra.*

Elizabeth knew all the important events transpiring within her kingdom. Sir Francis Walsingham, head of the secret service, on a number of occasions unearthed plots and intrigues, and hastened to tell his Queen the electrifying news only to discover she already knew more about the details than he did. That Elizabeth would appreciate the historical importance of Holinshed's *Chronicles,* and the classical and biographical importance of North's translation of *Plutarch's Lives,* is a foregone conclusion. An avid reader, she would not have waited for the publication of either Holinshed or North but would have read both works in manuscript. North dedicated *Plutarch's Lives* to Queen Elizabeth. He would have had to obtain her consent to the dedication and she would have had to read the *Lives* to judge of their merit before authorizing the dedication. North may have presented a copy of the manuscript to Elizabeth or she may have borrowed the copy held by the Stationers' Register. Elizabeth must have been fascinated by both Holinshed and North.

As we learned in chapter II, Shake-speare knew that she had won the Olympian olive crown for contemporary drama in 1591. She contemplated her climb to the top of the ladder of play perfection; her apprenticeship had started within a few months of the 1580 earthquake so that this eleven-year period mentioned in *Romeo and Juliet* was also the period of her dramatic labors. We may even know the exact date on which those labors commenced. The dual mention of "Lammas-eve at night" in *Romeo and Juliet* suggests the Lammas-eve preceding April 6, 1580, which would be August 1, 1579.

The earthquake, *Plutarch's Lives,* and *Timon of Athens* were all interrelated. The quake (i.e. shake) might have played some part in the selection of the pen name Shake-speare.

John Lyly's second novel, *Euphues and His England* was licensed on July 24, 1579. Within a day or two of that date, Simier, the French Ambassador and special envoy for the marriage proposals of the Duke of Alencon, in a fit of temper blurted out to Elizabeth the ghastly news of the secret marriage of Lord Leicester and Elizabeth's cousin, Lettice. Elizabeth was heartbroken. This cruel affront to her pride was probably the most severe emotional shock she would ever receive. She banished Lettice Knollys from her court and did not lay eyes on Lettice for many, many years. Leicester was placed under house arrest and almost went to the Tower.

In a melancholy mood, Elizabeth knew the best cure for grief was hard work. Her own bitterness turned her thoughts to a study of the classical embodiment of bitterness, *Timon of Athens*. She felt a kinship to Timon, whose best friends were also false, and in a mood to write his life: she turned to playwriting as an emotional outlet. Of all the Greek masters of the drama, Aristophanes probably appealed most to the tastes of Elizabeth and it is not surprising she should adopt Aristophanes as her first guide and consultant on play composition. The Queen, too soul-sick for comedy, adapted the satire of Aristophanes for tragedy. *Timon of Athens* has the form of a play but in reality is no play at all but an *oration on ingratitude*. The oration may be said to begin with the acrid philosophic utterances of Apemantus and it is here we see the resemblance to the style and spice of the comedy of Aristophanes. But the play, or oration, does not stay a comedy for long. Timon's friends show him the basest ingratitude. Timon renounces the world and goes to live in his seaside cave; he picks up the oration from Apemantus; pours forth pages of the most heart-rending invective bitterness. Such must have been the agonies of Elizabeth's mind when she lost Robert Dudley to another woman. To a play audience, the production would be oppressive and boring. As an *oration on ingratitude* it is a monument seldom if ever surpassed. Elizabeth worked on *Timon of Athens* in late 1579 and early 1580. Since this was her first dramatic effort she no doubt rewrote the play a number of times; perhaps the final version was prepared several years after 1580.

M. R. Ridley makes this comment of *Timon of Athens*, "It is a savage play. There is an unrelieved bitterness about it unique in Shakespeare's work. It seems the work of a man not only preoccupied with the topic of ingratitude much more certainly than the writer of *Lear*, but also utterly disillusioned." Ivor Brown says, "For its torrents of world-loathing and summoning of doom there can be nothing like it in English literature, not even in Shakespeare's masterpieces." Timon calls on Earth to:

"Ensear thy fertile and conceptious womb;
Let it no more bring out ingrateful man!
Go great with tigers, dragons, wolves and bears;
Teem with new monsters, whom thy upward face
Hath to the marbled mansion all above
Never presented!"

Ivor Brown's observations become even more pertinent, "So soaked is it in misanthropy, so embittered with sex obsession, that it may have been started, or worked upon, by Shakespeare in a mood verging upon nervous breakdown." . . . "That Timon should inveigh against ingratitude is natural; but why must he turn his frantic rhetoric upon the frailty of woman? There is no reason, except the anguish to which Shakespeare had been reduced by some overwhelming personal experience in which a faithless woman had played a devastating part."

Brown thinks this same faithless woman is personified not only in *Timon of Athens* but also in *Troilus and Cressida, Antony and Cleopatra,* and as the "dark lady" of the sonnets. Lettice Knollys fits the role perfectly. She was strongly suspected of having an affair with Dudley while her first husband was head of the English army in Ireland. The first Earl of Essex had died rather suddenly in Ireland in 1575 and it was rumored that he had been poisoned at the instigation of Leicester. While married to Dudley, Lettice was again unfaithful. This lover, Sir Christopher Blount, became the third husband of Lettice Knollys less than a year after the Earl of Leicester's death. Milton Waldman says of Elizabeth, "There was something positively fiendish in her desire to hurt and humiliate; a desire born out of her own hurt and humiliation, . . ." Elizabeth dubbed her cousin Lettice, "That she-wolf." Woman-like, Elizabeth blamed Lettice more than Robert and hated Lettice more than Robert. Hatred of a faithless woman who had stolen her man, was the perfect motivation for the fury of the "dark lady" sonnets as it was for the loathing and sex obsession of *Timon of Athens.*

There were several available sources for the story of Timon. Elizabeth probably had read the narrative first in Lucian's dialogue of *Timon or Misanthropos,* then in William Paynter's *Palace of*

Pleasure (1566). The immediate and working source was Plutarch's *Life of Antonius* and *Life of Alcibiades*. More than likely
Elizabeth had read Plutarch in the original or the translation into
French by Jacques Amyot. Sir Thomas North apparently published his English translation in January or February of 1580.
Shake-speare used both Aristophanes and Sophocles for dramatic
inspiration for *Timon of Athens*; act 4, scene 3, shows a strong
resemblance to the *Antigone*, 1344–45, of Sophocles.

The University of Cambridge established its first professorship
of Greek when Elizabeth was seven years of age. The introduction
of Greek learning and Greek literature to the schools of England
and to the Court of England, was one of the foundations upon
which the Reformation and the Renaissance was to rest. The im-
pact on the thinking and the dramatic tastes of the English was tre-
mendous. Without the Greek influence, the University Wits would
not have adopted free-lance writing as their avocation. The highest
form of Greek literature was the Greek play, so that playwriting
was bound to be the chief medium for literature of this period.
Elizabeth through Roger Ascham and her other classic tutors must
have had the greatest respect and admiration for the work of
Sophocles, Aristophanes, Aeschylus, and Euripides. Ascham specifically mentions the young Princess as studying the plays of
Sophocles. It seems an almost foregone conclusion that Elizabeth,
a born competitor and a learned scholar, would try her hand at the
most popular of indoor sports, the writing of drama, and because
of her admiration for the masterful Greek writers she was bound
to use them as a guide to her drama composition.

Less than a week after Simier's devastating news of the Dudley-Knollys nuptials, Queen Elizabeth, on July 29th, gave Edmund Tylney a writ of permanent appointment as Master of
Revels. He was to hold this all-important post for over thirty
years. The Master of Revels position had become vacant in March
1577 with the death of Sir Thomas Benger. Tylney had a temporary appointment in December of 1578. After a half-year trial
Elizabeth must have felt that Tylney was the kind of man she
could trust completely all the way to the grave. Elizabeth worked
in close conjunction with Tylney for the rest of her life. Every
play had to be passed upon by the Master of Revels. Tylney's first
act on receiving a new play was to transmit a copy of it to Eliza-

beth. Little wonder the charge of wholesale plagiarism is some-times laid at Shake-speare's door. Elizabeth felt a royal preroga-tive to use any idea that came her way, and all play ideas did come her way through Tylney. All can be forgiven for Shake-speare took bad plays and made them good, and good plays and made them excellent.

1580

The Queen's first contemporary dramatic guide was John Lyly. In 1580 the Queen entertained Lyly as "her servant" and in the same year she made him Master of the Children of St. Paul. Lyly abandoned the novel after *Euphues and His England* and devoted all his time to the writing of plays. He was soon known as the "Queen's dramatist." *The Woman in the Moon,* his one blank-verse play, and *Endymion* were written prior to 1580. From 1580 to 1583 appeared four more comedies of John Lyly, *Sappho and Phao, Gallathea, Alexander and Campaste,* and *Love's Metamor-phosis.* All six of these plays were first presented before the Queen's Majesty by the children of her choir and the children of St. Paul. Material derived from all six comedies appears in the comedies of Shake-speare.

According to Ashley H. Thorndike, Lyly, "is partly respon-sible for the spread of the epidemic of puns, word plays and con-ceits that infected Elizabethan comedy, but he is also credited with its gain in lightness, ease and fancy." . . . His plays, ". . . con-stitute the first original English type of comedy, and they provided a model and method for Shakespeare."

Lyly tried hard to obtain the job of Master of Revels. While the Queen showed him many favors she did not grant this one. Apparently she thought Tylney was more to be trusted than Lyly.

In 1580, Shake-speare wrote *Pericles,* probably commenced in the first half of the year. Leicester was in semi-banishment until July of 1580, when a final reconciliation took place. Ingratitude was one of the central themes of *Pericles* reflecting continued bitter-ness over the Dudley-Knollys marriage. *Pericles* has all the ele-ments of Greek tragedy but death; ingratitude, incest, shipwreck, envy, bondage, wanderings over the Mediterranean. Perhaps best classed as a tragi-comedy because it insists on a happy ending, the play gives one the sense of strain. Too much is attempted, too little accomplished. *Pericles* has all the dramatic situations one could possibly ask for but the various plots and counterplots do not dovetail harmoniously. The play is unwieldy, it lacks unity and cohesion; it is exactly the kind of play that would be the first or second attempt of a gifted writer still struggling with his style and characterization. If *Timon of Athens* be considered an oration, then *Pericles* could be called the first real play. That *Pericles* is an amateurish production every line proclaims; that it could not possibly follow *Hamlet, Macbeth*, and *Lear* in chronological order is too apparent for further comment.

Pericles and the three comedies which follow *Pericles* were tragi-comedies. Shake-speare was attempting an original type play. Shake-speare's natural element was comedy but she wished to write comedy in a more serious vein. The attempt was a failure and after these four plays she abandoned her efforts at tragi-comedy in favor of straight comedy. She put her ideas of originality in the background and leaned more heavily upon the methods and mannerisms of John Lyly and George Peele.

1581

In 1581 Thomas Newton translated Seneca's plays into English blank verse.

In 1581 the Privy Council gave the Master of Revels general power over the whole of England not only to license individual plays but to "order and reform, authorize and put down, all plays, players and playmakers, together with their playing parts." Tylney was given the power to commit offenders to prison.

In 1581 Shake-speare wrote *Measure for Measure*. The structure of the play was crude like *Pericles*. *Measure for Measure* was extensively revised and rewritten about twenty years after the first draft, so that it contains mature material hung upon its youthful framework. We have already noted the source of *Measure for Measure* as *Promos and Cassandra* written three years prior to 1581 by George Whetstone.

1582

Our list has *Cymbeline* and *The Tempest* as composed in 1582. *The Tempest* has no known source and must be classed as an original. *Cymbeline* used allusions to the old British king, Cymbeline,

found in Holinshed. Boccaccio's *Decameron* (day 2, novel 9)
furnished the story of Imogen. *Cymbeline* has much in common
with *Pericles*; the scene has shifted from the Mediterranean to the
British Isles but the marvelous revelations and miraculous escapes
from death are similar strains in both plays. *Cymbeline* is an advance over *Pericles* because the complex intermixture of plots is
better handled in the British play. *Cymbeline* shows more indi-
cations of the influence of John Lyly. The lark song in *Cymbeline*,
act 2, scene 3:

> "Hark! Hark! the lark at heaven's gate sings,
> And Phoebus 'gins arise."

is taken from Trico's speech in act 5, scene 1, of *Alexander and
Campaste*:

> "Brave pricksong! Who is't now we hear?
> None but the lark so shrill and clear;
> Now at heaven's gate she claps her wings,
> And morn not waking till she sings."

The Tempest is a transition piece between tragi-comedy and
comedy, for it may be classed as either. The audience is fully prepared for the tragedy that is synonymous with shipwreck, yet the
magical powers of Prospero which caused the storm at sea are such
as to forbid all loss of life; so the tragi-comedy becomes a comedy.
The elves and spirits of *The Tempest* are drawn from John Lyly's
comedies. Shake-speare has renounced originality and has a new
goal; she will exploit Lyly's genius to the utmost and improve on
said genius in due course. Shake-speare now fully realizes that
tragedy and comedy will not mix, she will henceforth write comic
comedy, witty comedy, word-play comedy, and classic comedy. The
serious subjects of chronicle-play and tragedy would bye and bye be
dealt with in a serious vein, some comedy relief, of course, but no
halving of tragic and comic motif. The one exception, *The Winter's Tale*, will be explained in the next chapter.

1583 ▾

1583 was a year of firsts for Shake-speare. She wrote her first
long poem, *Venus and Adonis*; her first true comedy, *The Taming
of A Shrew*, which was also her first play to reach the stage (1588);

and her first history play, *King Henry VIII*, which she designed to be her last play to reach the stage (1613). When Shake-speare in the dedication called *Venus and Adonis*, "the first heir of my invention," she might have signified her first work deemed to merit publication. Apparently Shake-speare discarded her first five plays as not stageworthy, although years later she did revise *Measure for Measure*.

Elizabeth all her life was the soul of patience. As we have seen, many of her important political triumphs came as the result of the fact that she could outwait her opponents. She did not expect a masterpiece on the first or second dramatic attempt or perhaps even on the ninth or tenth. She just kept right on trying. When she did write a play which demanded an audience, she would in good time put it on the stage. *Timon of Athens* was largely the outpourings of wounded pride; once she had finished the oration-play she felt better. The next four plays were in an original genre which proved to be an experimental failure and at length all five plays were abandoned in favor of the style of Lyly.

The Taming of A Shrew, revised in the 1590's as *The Taming of The Shrew*, is a lively and pleasing spectacle. The female characters in *The Taming of The Shrew* take on lifelike characteristics in contrast to the puppet-simplicity of the women in the first five plays. Shake-speare has arrived at a firm foundation; she has found the proper path to dramatic maturity to be the improvement of the best work of her fellow playwrights.

The authorities on Shake-speare make the statement that the author must have used the second edition of Holinshed published in 1587, ten years after the appearance of the first edition. The second edition was brought up to date, with additions to and some rewording of the old material. The wording of the second edition of Holinshed (in contrast to the first edition) is in evidence in most of the history plays. This, however, is not true of *Cymbeline*, *Lear*, or *Henry VIII*. *King Henry VIII* has four sources, Hall's *Union of the Families of Lancaster and York* (1548), Holinshed's *Chronicles*, John Stow's *The Annals of England* (1580), and Foxe's *Acts and Monuments of the Church* (1563). The simplest and least mature of the history plays, *Henry VIII* retains more of Holinshed's actual wording than any other play. For these reasons it must have been Shake-speare's first effort at epic chronicle play composition.

Henry VIII is written exactly as Queen Elizabeth would write it. The play ends with the birth and baptism of Elizabeth. In the play, the Queen Dowager, Catherine of Aragon, dies before Elizabeth's birth (contrary to history) which resolves (dramatically) any possible taint of illegitimacy. By ending the play in 1533, she spares her father the unfortunate acts which have given him the nickname of Bluebeard. The play is a memorial to her mother. Anna Jameson says, "How completely, in the few paragraphs appropriated to Anne Bullen, is her character portrayed. With what a delicate and yet luxuriant grace is she sketched off, with her beauty, her levity, her extreme mobility, her sweetness of disposition, her tenderness of heart. . . ."

In 1583 Francis Walsingham ordered Edmund Tylney to select the best players from the different companies then in existence to form one predominant company to be known as the "Queen's Men." Between 1583 and 1590, the "Queen's Men" gave twenty-one of the thirty adult performances chosen for the court.

1584

To 1584 have been assigned *The Comedy of Errors* and the long poem *The Rape of Lucrece*. *The Comedy of Errors* is a delightful comedy, not mature but maturing. *The Comedy of Errors* had to be written between 1584 and 1589 because of the reference to the King of Navarre being heir to the French throne in the geographical description of the kitchen wench in act 3, scene 2:

"Antipholus of Syracuse: 'Where France?'
"Dromio of Syracuse: 'In her forehead; armed and reverted,
                          making war against her heir.' "

The King of Navarre became heir to the French throne in 1584 with the death of Francis, Duke of Alencon-Anjou (Elizabeth's last suitor), and ceased to be the heir when he became the King of France as well as King of Navarre in 1589, when Henry III was murdered.

Perhaps the most significant event of 1584 was the presentation before Queen Elizabeth of George Peele's *The Arrangement of Paris* by the Children of the Chapel Royal. Peele possessed an exquisite feeling for the musical sound of words. M. M. Reese says, ". . . without the lyrical freshness of Peele he (Shake-speare) would not have interspersed his plays with songs, . . ."

1585

Shake-speare did not wait long to adopt the beauty of Peele's word magic to her own uses. The next play, *Love's Labour's Lost* (1585) is full of songs and delightful sonnets. All the Shake-speare comedies from and including *Love's Labour's Lost* show repeated evidence of the influence of George Peele.

Mr. John Schick tells us that Thomas Kyd's *The Spanish Tragedy* was probably written between 1583 and 1585, making full use of Thomas Newton's translation into English of the Seneca plays (1581). Mr. Schick comments, "If we add that here, for the first time, a successful fusion of classic and national elements has been brought about on a great scale, we shall not hesitate to say that Kyd's play represents a mighty intellectual and artistic effort for its time."

Shake-speare's indebtedness to Kyd is most manifest in *Titus Andronicus* (1585), a similar tale of horror and blood-bath to *The Spanish Tragedy*. In many Shake-speare plays we see evidence that Shake-speare followed Kyd in a number of devices of play construction; in the manipulation of plot and in the exploitation of effective situations.

1586

Leslie Hotson has identified *Loves' Labour's Won* as *Troilus and Cressida*. We would expect *Love's Labour's Lost* and *Love's Labour's Won* to follow one another in chronological order and we have assigned *Love's Labour's Lost* to 1585 and *Troilus and Cressida* to 1586. *Love's Labour's Lost* and *Troilus and Cressida* defy comparison but invite contrast. *Love's Labour's Lost* ends with the French Princess and her three beautiful companions requesting the King of Navarre and his three handsome nobles (because the four young men have broken an oath to shun the company of ladies) to undertake one year's work for humanity; thereupon the four ladies will entertain the four gentlemen as suitors. Love is lost for only the period of a year's labor for mankind. After the elapse of the year we can visualize the successful conclusion of the four love affairs.

In *Love's Labour's Won* Troilus wins Cressida; they become lovers after a short romance. However, Cressida has a roving eye and is soon warm to the advances of Diomedes. The love won by Troilus is as empty as air.

Ulysses says of Cressida:

> "Fie, fie upon her!
> There's language in her eye, her cheek, her lip,
> Nay, her foot speaks; her wanton spirits look out
> At every joint and motive of her body."

Cressida perceives her own weakness in a brief soliloquy:

> "Troilus, farewell! one eye yet looks on thee,
> But with my heart the other eye doth see."

Of whom does Cressida and her wanton character remind us? We see in Cressida the same personality as the Dark Lady of the Sonnets. We would expect *Troilus and Cressida* to have been written at about the same time as the Dark Lady Sonnets and I have listed the date as 1586. Butler has placed the writing of the Dark Lady Sonnets as about 1585–86.

There is a connection also between *Love's Labour's Lost* and the Dark Lady Sonnets. Lord Berowne (Biron) loves Rosaline, who is a dark beauty.

> "King: 'O paradox! Black is the badge of hell,
> The hue of dungeons and the scowl of night;
> And beauty's crest becomes the heavens well.'

> "Berowne: 'Devils soonest tempt, resembling spirits of light,
> O! if in black my lady's brows be deck'd,
> It mourns that painting and usurping hair
> Should ravish doters with a false aspect;
> And therefore is she born to make black fair.' "

T. W. Baldwin comments of *Love's Labour's Lost* and the Dark Lady Sonnets, "So for Sonnet 127 Shakespeare has simply and solely put Biron's (Berowne's) paradoxical black beauty into sonnet form. She began as a literary paradox; in the sonnets, at least, she never becomes anything more . . . The black beauty is always presented jestingly, though, of course, her lover always takes her seriously . . . Certainly, then, one should not be surprised at any of the antithetical and paradoxical things which are done to her; they are a part of the definitely indicated plan . . . There is no indication that the mistress is black or for that matter any other color."

Since we have listed the Dark Lady Sonnets as being written the year after the composition of *Love's Labour's Lost*, we in a way have added plausibility to Baldwin's theory that the Dark Lady Sonnets were merely exercises in the sonnet form. Although these sonnets might be partly dramatic or partly allegorical, the personality of the Dark Lady was not written out of an imaginative void. Shake-speare had some definite female acquaintance in mind. The hatred and jealousy expressed against the Dark Lady was too vivid and too bitter not to be related to some personal emotional experience.

In December of 1585, Robert Dudley, Earl of Leicester, had departed for the Low Countries to command the English armies against Spain. Dudley had been specifically instructed by the Queen not to accept any titles from their Dutch allies. Nevertheless, Leicester allowed himself to be commissioned as Governor-General of The Netherlands. The Queen had not declared war on Spain and wished her connection with the Dutch to stay as far in the background as possible, so that the action of Robert Dudley was most embarrassing. On February 10, 1586 Elizabeth sent the following letter to Dudley:

> "How contemptuously we conceive ourself to have been used by you, you shall by this bearer understand, whom we have expressly sent to you to charge you withal. We could never have imagined, had we not seen it fall out in experience, that a man raised up by ourself, and extraordinarily favoured by us above any other subject of this land, would have in so contemptible a sort have broken our commandment, in a cause that so greatly toucheth us in honour, whereof, although you have showed yourself to make but little account, in most undutiful a sort, you may not therefore think that we have so little care of the reparation thereof as we mind to pass so great a wrong in silence unredressed: and, therefore, our express pleasure and command is, all delays and excuses laid apart, you do presently, upon the duty of your allegiance, obey and fulfill whatsoever the bearer hereof shall direct you to do in our name: whereof fail you not, as you will answer the contrary at your uttermost peril."

To make matters worse Elizabeth learned that Lady Leicester, the hated cousin Lettice, was about to join her Governor-General husband, "with such a train of ladies and gentlemen and such coaches, litters and side saddles, as her Majesty had none such, and that there should be such a court of ladies as should surpass her Majesty's court here." Milton Waldman asserts that Queen Elizabeth was "Beside herself with fury, coupling the name of 'that she-wolf' and her errant lover 'with great oaths' she swore she 'would have no more courts under her obeisance than her own.'" Waldman says of the bad blood between Elizabeth and Lettice, ". . . one cause of Elizabeth's unforgiving hostility was the suspicion that Lettice had betrayed the man Elizabeth had loved and lost to her" for a younger man, Sir Christopher Blount.

Lettice Knollys is the Dark Lady of the Sonnets. In 1586 Elizabeth had a new grudge against Robert Dudley and especially against Lettice Knollys. Employing Dudley as her mouthpiece, Elizabeth tells Leicester's story in Sonnets 127–152. She makes Dudley heap shame on the head of Lettice and admit his own weakness and lack of character. Dudley states that Lettice has broken her bed-vow with her first husband for him and now she is doing the same thing to Dudley with other men. In spite of this Dudley admits that he still loves Lettice and cannot break her spell. Had Shake-speare been a male he would have blackened his name as a fool and worse with the Dark Lady Sonnets, and would have been guilty of offending all the rules of masculine chivalry. For Elizabeth to use this literary outlet for her emotions is quite in keeping with feminine psychology. You ladies who have lost a good man to a hussy, could you find better words to describe this hussy than these extracts from the Dark Lady Sonnets:

"In nothing art thou black save in thy deeds,"

"I do believe her though I know she lies"

"Robb'd others' beds' revenues of their rents"

"The worser spirit a woman, colour'd ill."

"For I have sworn thee fair and thought thee bright,
Who art as black as hell, and dark as night."

"For I have sworn thee fair: more perjur'd I,
To swear against the truth so foul a lie."

"Be anchor'd in the bay where all men ride," . . .

By 1586 Elizabeth had fashioned an appropriate pen name.
We have already called attention to the fact that in a speech to
Parliament in that year she had said, ". . . Then to the end I
might make the better progress in the art of *swaying the sceptre* I
entered into long and serious cogitation what things were worthy
and fitting for kings to do; . . ."

SWAYING-THE-SCEPTRE
SHAKE-THE-SPEARE
SHAKE-SPEARE

In 1588 the nine years writing apprenticeship suggested by
Horace would be over. Elizabeth had a tragedy, *Titus Andronicus*
and a comedy, *The Taming of A Shrew* to place upon the stage.
For 1589 she had *The Comedy of Errors* and *Love's Labour's
Lost*. She needed a living, breathing, masculine embodiment for
her nom de plume, Shake-speare. In 1587 she instructed Edmund
Tylney, who in turn instructed someone in the Queen's company of
actors that while on tour in the provinces to be on the lookout for
a potential actor with a name like Shake-speare. Ivor Brown picks
up the story, "Perhaps 1587 was the deciding date. The Queen's
Men, with Tarleton and Kempe as Chief Clowns were in Warwickshire at midsummer. This was the company he (Shakespeare)
was later to serve and to grace."

Chapter X

TIME-SCALE PARALLELS

"There is a point, to which when men aspire,
They tumble headlong down: That point I touch'd,
And, seeing there was no place to mount higher,
Why should I grieve at my declining fall?
Farewell, fair queen: weep not for Mortimer,
That scorns the world, and, as a traveler,
Goes to discover countries yet unknown."

Edward II—Christopher Marlowe

A. W. Pollard states, ". . . On this view the plays which show the most classical influence, *Titus*, *Errors* and the *Shrew*, would be the real products of his work-shop days, and despite verse tests or any other evidence of the kind I should like to see them assigned to the earliest possible dates." We have *Titus*, *Errors*, and the *Shrew* included in our first eleven plays. Of the eleven plays listed as written between 1579 and 1586, inclusive, most of them lean heavily on the classics—certainly the first play, *Timon of Athens* with its scene in ancient Greece and the last, *Troilus and Cressida*, which is built upon incidents in Homer's *Iliad*.

We have already noted that *Troilus and Cressida* (1586) could be called a prologue to the history plays. Shake-speare took up the writing of the epic chronicle play as her major activity during 1587 and 1588 when the three parts of *Henry VI* and the play of *Richard III* were composed. Since Christopher Marlowe was considered to be the collaborator of the *Henry VI* plays with Shake-speare, let us take a look at Marlowe's endeavors at this time.

Christopher Marlowe was born in Canterbury in 1564. He was two months older than William Shakspere. John Marlowe, Christopher's father, was a maker of shoes, a member of the Shoemaker's Craft, a churchwarden and a parish clerk. In January 1579, Christopher Marlowe entered King's School, Canterbury, on one of fifty scholarships maintained for boys between the ages of nine and fifteen. Two years later he applied for admission to Corpus Christi College, Cambridge, on a six-year scholarship, created by the will of Archbishop Parker of Canterbury. A candidate for the scholarship had to be able to read music, sing, and compose verse. At seventeen, Marlowe was already a poet. His sojourn at Cambridge was from December 1580 until June 1587, in which time, besides attending the lectures of a divinity student, he translated much of Ovid, translated the first book of Lucan's *Pharsalia*, wrote *The Tragedy of Dido*, and most if not all of both parts of *Tamburlaine, the Great*. *Dido* was performed before Her Majesty in May 1587 and both part 1 and part 2 of *Tamburlaine* were on the stage not later than November of 1587.

Marlowe received his B.A. in 1584 but when he petitioned for his M.A. in the spring of 1587, the University demurred on the grounds that Marlowe had been absent too much. Marlowe sought royal aid and it was not long coming in the form of a stern letter, dated June 26, 1587, from the Privy Council signed by the Lord Archbishop, the Lord Chancellor, the Lord Treasurer, the Lord Chamberlain, and Her Majesty's Comptroller, which recited:

> "Whereas, it was reported that Christopher Marlowe was determined to have gone beyond the seas to Rheims and there remain, their Lordships thought good to certify that he had no such intent but that in all his actions he had behaved himself orderly and discreetly whereby he had done her Majesty good service, and deserved to be rewarded for his faithful dealing: Their Lordships request was that the rumor thereof should be allayed by all possible means, and he should be furthered in the degree he was to take this next Commencement: because it was not her Majesty's pleasure that anyone employed as he had been in matters touching the benefit of his Country should be defamed by those that are ignorant in the affairs he went about."

Needless to say, Mr. Marlowe was awarded his M.A. This letter did not say that Marlowe had been at Rheims or anywhere else and it gave no hint as to what services he had performed for his Queen. Normally a writer is employed to write so that we are bound to guess that he was helping her Majesty draft *Henry VI*. The buttery (food provisions) records of Cambridge show that Marlowe was absent more than half of the time during the academic year 1584–85, in regular attendance during the year 1585–86 and again absent much more than half of the time in 1586–87. In 1586–87 he attended only part of the first and part of the second term and was absent all the third and fourth terms. In 1584–85 his services may have been procured to work on *Titus Andronicus* since some authorities credit him with part authorship in this bloody tragedy. A number of authorities contend that Marlowe labored only on parts 2 and 3 of *King Henry VI*, while others see his hand in all three parts. There is internal evidence that he worked on *1 Henry VI*. The prologue to *1 Tamburlaine* has a line:

"Threatening the world with high astounding terms"

1 Henry VI, act 1, scene 2, Charles, the Dauphin, says to Joan of Arc:

"Thou hast astonish'd me with thy high terms,"

The academic year 1586–87 seems to have been devoted by Marlowe to helping draft all three parts of *Henry VI*. The collaboration of Elizabeth and Christopher Marlowe may have continued through 1587 and on into 1588.

Christopher Marlowe was interested solely in tragedy; he wrote no comedies. His one chronicle play, *Edward II*, was picked for its high tragedy. Marlowe lacked the common touch and the fine spice of humor so manifest in Shake-speare, and Marlowe also lacked the artistry of painting lifelike women so well developed in Robert Greene and in mature Shake-speare. He was never able to put the breath of reality into his feminine characters even in his mature work. His Abigail in *The Jew of Malta* and his Isabella in *Edward II* were little more than puppets and the strength his *Dido* possessed she already had in the poetry of the *Fourth Aeneid*. John Symonds remarked, "But it was precisely on the side of humour that Marlowe showed his chief inferiority to Shakespeare. That saving grace of the dramatic poet he lacked altogether. And it may also be parenthetically noticed as significant in this respect that Marlowe never drew a woman's character." Yet the spirit and eloquence of Marlowe's "mighty line" was the strongest ingredient to be amalgamated into Shake-speare's "mighty line" in the composition of Shake-speare's mature history and mature tragedy.

Shake-speare eulogized Marlowe in *As You Like It*, act 3,

scene 5, when she used a line from Marlowe's *Hero and Leander*:

"Dead shepherd, now I find thy saw of might:
'Who ever loved that loved not at first sight?' "

The "rival poet" of the Sonnets is probably Christopher Marlowe. Elizabeth would not have honored any poet of less stature than Marlowe or Edmund Spenser, and the phraseology in Sonnet 86 suggests Marlowe. We know Elizabeth, Essex, and Marlowe must have been together in 1587 since both men were frequently with Elizabeth in that year.

Shake-speare's *The Winter's Tale* which we have listed as written in 1588, has for its source the novel *Pandosto* by Robert Greene. *Pandosto* was a popular novel and ran through many editions. In the 1588 edition of *Pandosto* the oracle gave this message, ". . . the king *shall live* without an heir if . . ." All later editions of *Pandosto* stated, ". . . the king *shall die* without an heir if . . ." Shake-speare used the "shall live" version, which caused P. G. Thomas to observe, "On the other hand, the fact that Shakespeare adopts this form of the oracle (*Winter's Tale*, 3, 2, 135) points to his having used the edition of 1588 or an earlier one, if such existed." Thomas did not indicate why he thought there might have been an earlier edition of *Pandosto*. Greene's main period of novel composition was 1580–84. After the appearance of Marlowe's *Tamburlaine, the Great*, in 1587, Greene devoted his energies principally to drama for the next few years. *Pandosto* might have had an earlier edition than the 1588 edition and *The Winter's Tale* might also have been written earlier than 1588.

Because Shake-speare followed the plot of *Pandosto* closely she had to write the story as both a tragedy and a comedy. In *The Winter's Tale*, the first three acts are tragedy, the last two acts are pastoral comedy. A chorus, spoken by Time, joins the two portions of the play and accounts for the sixteen-year interval between the end of the action of the tragedy and the beginning of the action of the comedy. The combination of tragedy and comedy is awkward; after due deliberation Shake-speare decided to discard *The Winter's Tale* as not stageworthy.

The last chronicle play of the 1587–88 quartet, *Richard III*, was perverted from history. Shake-speare made Richard a complete villian, who gloried in evil for its own sake apart from its results. Richard III was the foe of Elizabeth's grandfather, the Earl of Richmond and afterwards King Henry VII, at the battle of Bosworth. Elizabeth painted her grandfather the righteous, flawless hero, and his enemy, Richard, as a dastardly and flawless villian. Both Holinshed and Hall related how Richard disclosed to his followers remorse for the murder of his nephews:

> " 'And although in the adeption and obtaining of the garland, I being seduced and provoked by sinister council and diabolical temptation, did commit a wicked and detestable act, yet I have with strict penance and salt tears (as I trust) expiated and clearly purged the same offense: which abominable crime I require you of friendship as clearly to forget, as I daily remember to deplore and lament the same.' "

Elizabeth not only made no use of this evidence of remorse on Richard's part but created a contrary impression by the line of pure fiction she made Richard speak:

"Let not our babbling dreams affright our souls;"

The "lovely boy" sonnets (1–126) have been shown to have been written between April 1587 and the close of the year 1589. Since the Elizabeth and Essex romance flourished during this period of time and all the physical characteristics of the lovely boy fit Essex, we have judged Robert Devereux, Earl of Essex, to be the lovely boy. This makes the lovely mother of Sonnet 3, Lettice Knollys:

"Thou art thy mother's glass, and she in thee
Calls back the lovely April of her prime;"

Elizabeth loved Robert Devereux but she went right on hating his mother. The above lines are a compliment to the boy but not to his mother; the "of her prime" phrase ruins the compliment to the mother as Elizabeth had intended.

After the completion of *Richard III*, 1588, 1589, and 1590 were occupied by the sonnets and the four comedies, *The Winter's Tale* (unless it was written earlier than 1588), *The Two Gentlemen of Verona*, *A Midsummer Night's Dream*, and *Much Ado*

About Nothing. Late in 1590 the romance went smash when Essex married the widow of Sir Philip Sidney. In 1591 Shake-speare's mood for comedy changed to a mood for tragedy and she wrote *Romeo and Juliet*, the first tragedy since *Titus Andronicus*. As we know, *Romeo and Juliet* was written at the time of the unhappy ending of a love affair for Shake-speare. With the completion of *Romeo and Juliet*, Shake-speare had reached dramatic maturity and with the exception of the frothy *The Merry Wives of Windsor*, her plays for the dozen years she was to live, were all mature. There is a historical record of Elizabeth making translations of Horace and other Latin writers in the 1590's as a race against time. The translations were made in an incredibly short space of hours. These translations were not of high quality, which is mute testimony to the haste of the composition. There is a legend that Queen Elizabeth, after viewing a performance of *King Henry IV*, ordered Shake-speare to prepare a play within a fortnight showing Falstaff in love; i.e., she bet herself she could write such a play in two weeks. The haste of composition of *The Merry Wives of Windsor* make it an inferior production.

Elizabeth, we know from history, was exceedingly fond of composing riddles and epigrams. The type of sonnet chosen by Shake-speare ended in a detached rhymed couplet, which could scarcely avoid being epigrammatic. Shake-speare used numerous riddles in her plays. A good example will be found in *The Merchant of Venice*, with the riddle of the three caskets. Just another illustration of twinning, this fondness of epigrams and riddles by Shake-speare and Elizabeth.

Some of Elizabeth's poetry, written about 1581 or 1582 has been preserved. This poetry is neither good nor bad; its quality is about on a par with the poetic level of *Venus and Adonis* and *The Rape of Lucrece*, which we have thought might belong to about the same period (1583–84). During the years from 1579 to 1586 the improvement of writing skill came slowly for Elizabeth. Her association with Christopher Marlowe about 1586 and 1587 seems to have inspired her to grasp maturity. But if Marlowe encouraged Elizabeth to loftier heights, it is equally reasonable to suppose that Elizabeth inspired Marlowe to dramatic grandeur. There was a mutual debt in Marlowe's "mighty line" as there was in Shake-speare's "mighty line." The period, 1587–91, was a period of realization and fulfillment; Elizabeth's love for Essex during this time was instrumental in bringing beauty to the main body of the sonnets and penetration to the plays.

Elizabeth's self peeps out from several of her heroines. We see the Queen in Juliet, Portia, Beatrice, Rosalind, Viola, and Cassandra. Cassandra was gifted with the power of prophecy; when she repulsed Apollo's advances, Apollo brought it to pass that no one believed her predictions, although they were invariably correct. This all-wise demi-goddess, who could spurn the handsomest of the gods, was of a mold of kinship to Elizabeth. Cassandra was the appropriate personality to speak the immortal line of the "Imperial Votaress" in *Troilus and Cressida*:

> *"It is the purpose that makes strong the vow;"*

All of these heroines resemble Elizabeth in possessing beauty, wisdom, charm, mature judgment, balance, courage, bright wit, and sparkling humor. All of these heroines, like Elizabeth, knew what they wanted and proceeded to secure same. Almost every principal Shake-speare feminine character was in some part Elizabeth, and reacted to fate just as any noble woman might react under the circumstances.

The psychic urge that made Elizabeth place Portia, Rosalind, and Viola in men's clothing as a matter of disguise, might partially explain her motivation in disguising her own authorship in masculine raiment.

For every strong and mature Shake-speare heroine we have a weak, vacillating, impetuous hero. There is hesitating Hamlet; madly jealous Othello; flattery blinded Lear; Coriolanus, who like Essex, though a brave warrior is dominated by his mother. Who are these heroes but the embodiment of all the slow-thinking, impulsive, headstrong men of immature judgment who filled the English Court? These heroes are the princes, ambassadors, courtiers, and lovers with whom Elizabeth had crossed swords. In none of them had she found a mental equal—few were even tolerably exemplary; so that it is not surprising that there are no really heroic heroes in Shake-speare. George Bernard Shaw comments, "Thirty-six plays in five blank verse acts, and (as Mr. Ruskin, I think, once pointed out) not a single hero!"

Since both the Sonnet Folio of 1609 and the Play Folio of 1623 have been shown to be connected with the Pembroke family, we need to know what history reveals about the relationship between Queen Elizabeth and the Pembrokes. Mary Sidney (1561–1621) was the third daughter of Sir Henry Sidney. When her third and last sister died at the family home in Wales in 1575, Queen Elizabeth suggested that Mary join the royal household away from the unhealthful climate of Wales. Mary was gracious and kind as well as beautiful and soon won the hearts of the court. With her mother and her famous poet brother, Philip, she accompanied the Queen on a trip through Staffordshire and Worcester in the fall of 1575. Mary Sidney married Henry Herbert, second Earl of Pembroke, in 1577 and their first child, William, was born April 8, 1580. Francis Meres called Mary ". . . a most delicate poet." She was joint author with her brother of a book of Psalms, published a poem in Edmund Spenser's *Astrophel* in 1595, and revised some of her brother's work on *Arcadia*. She had also written a play about 1592 called *The Tragedy of Antonie*.

A lifelong friend of Queen Elizabeth, Mary Herbert, with her fine education and literary skill, was the natural choice for the trust of preserving and publishing the plays and the sonnets. Late in 1599, Elizabeth honored the Countess of Pembroke with a visit to Wilton, beautiful Pembroke home-place. It was a quiet visit and history almost missed the event; a letter which made its appearance many years later, told of the episode. This almost secret visit was a perfect occasion for Elizabeth to present the Shakespeare manuscripts to Mary Herbert for safekeeping. *Hamlet*, which Elizabeth probably considered her masterpiece, was finished that year. The Countess of Pembroke was given the sonnet manuscripts and all of the play manuscripts except *Othello*, *Macbeth*, and *Lear*, which were not to be written until 1600, 1601, and 1602.

Elizabeth's instructions to Mary Herbert were precise. The Sonnets were to be published in ten years. *King Henry VIII* was to be placed on the stage exactly ten years after Elizabeth's death in a month midway between the month of her death and the month of her birth. The publication of the full body of her plays was to be exactly twenty years after her death. The William Shakspere myth was to be preserved. Certain unproduced plays were to be put on the stage in such and such years. Revision of *Henry VIII* so as to incorporate in it allusions to current history was to be done by Mary Herbert. As Elizabeth was to leave to her women the preparation of her body for burial so did she leave to a woman the destiny of her literary efforts.

Actually the trust was in the entire Pembroke family. Young William Herbert had an hour's private audience with Elizabeth in that November visit of 1599. Elizabeth no doubt left some of the burden of preservation on young Herbert and on his brother,   x Philip, to whom the First Play Folio was jointly dedicated. Elizabeth left instructions that the Sonnet Folio and the Play Folio were to be dedicated to the Pembrokes.

In September of 1599, two months before this visit to Wilton, the Earl of Essex had suddenly returned from Ireland against orders, deserting his post as Lord Lieutenant of Ireland, and had suffered arrest and disgrace. The heroes of the Roman plays *Coriolanus* and *Antony and Cleopatra* were men somewhat similar in their mistakes and their shortcomings to Robert Devereux, and the stage production of these two plays was probably delayed for roughly ten years in deference to Essex. There was usually a lapse of some four or five years between the writing and production of the Shake-speare plays, and for *Othello*, *Macbeth*, and *Lear* to be written in 1600, 1601, and 1602 and produced in 1604, 1606, and 1606 seems logical. *King Lear* has been judged to be the product of a period of gloom in Shake-speare's life. 1602, the year of composition, coming after the execution of Essex for treason, was a year of deep melancholia for Queen Elizabeth. This mental disturbance probably hastened her death.

The Countess of Pembroke wrote a letter to her son William in 1604 stating that "that fellow Shakspere" was at Wilton, and urged her son to bring King James to Wilton for a stage performance. If Mary Herbert and William Herbert, her son, had not both been aware that William Shakspere was not the author Shake-speare, she would never have referred to the actor as "that   x fellow Shakspere." Mary Herbert would have had the highest respect and admiration for the writer Shake-speare.

When the year 1609 dawned and it was time to have the Sonnet Folio printed, William Herbert (Mr. W. H.) took the manuscripts to the publisher Thorpe. Probably the Countess of Pembroke wrote the ambiguous Sonnet dedication. If Thomas Thorpe wrote the dedication he was instructed to designate the begetter only as Mr. W. H. Since Queen Elizabeth had been forced to have the head of her "lovely boy" cut off for treason in 1601, the identity of the "lovely boy" had to be obscured by a misleading dedication which would deceive and bewilder rather than instruct.

Prior to 1613, Mary Herbert changed *King Henry VIII* to indicate allusions to the reign of James I; other plays including *Macbeth* might have been altered likewise. *Henry VIII* was placed on the stage in June 1613 according to Elizabeth's instructions. The Countess of Pembroke worked on the preparation of the First Play Folio during 1619, 1620, and 1621. The Folio started to press in mid-April of 1621 and was on the bookstands in 1623 in obedience to the instructions of Queen Elizabeth.

Elizabeth Tudor's Life Cycle Number was ten. Her birth date was September 7, 1533.

September	9
Date	7
Year	1533
Total	1549

1 plus 5 plus 4 plus 9 equals 19
1 plus 9 equals 10

This computation had to be made from the Julian calendar, or the old English calendar, or the Gregorian calendar of 1582 since in the sixteenth century the English New Year started on March 25. We moderns might ignore such a thing as a Life Cycle Number as superstition; not so the Elizabethans. Queen Elizabeth had seen the number ten turn up in her life too often not to be aware of the power of the "Never-tiring holy ten" of Pythagoras.

Both of the Queen's favorites, the two Roberts, had possessed feet of clay. Both had given her moments of great happiness and moments of the bitterest heartache. All-powerful as she was, Elizabeth knew full well that she lived in a man's world:

"Isabella: '. . . : but man, proud man,
Drest in a little brief authority,
Most ignorant of what he's most assured,
His glassy essence, like an angry ape,
Plays such fantastic tricks before high heaven,
As make the angels weep: . . .' "

Measure for Measure

Even a great Queen had to battle male prejudice all her life. The hardest fight was on the battlefield of male literary bias where the main offensive would take place after death, when her superior intellect could no longer thrust and parry in her defense. If Mary Ann Evans Cross had good reason to write *Silas Marner* and *Mill on the Floss* as George Eliot, and Charlotte Bronte thought it wise to compose *Jane Eyre* and *Wuthering Heights* as Curren Bell, what could be more logical than for Elizabeth to let Shake-speare be her pen name and leave as her final clue the dramatization of the history of her father, her mother, and her baby self as her last play on the stage, with the riddle of the epilogue as the key to the mystery.

> " 'Tis ten to one this play can never please
> All that are here: some come to take their ease,
> And sleep an act or two; but those, we fear,
> We have frighted with our trumpets; so 'tis clear,
> They'll say 'tis naught: others, to hear the city
> Abused extremely, and to cry 'That's witty!'
> Which we have not done neither: that, I fear
> All the expected good we're like to hear
> For this play at this time, is only in
> The merciful construction of good women;
> For such a one we show'd 'em: if they smile,
> And say 'twill do, I know, within a while
> All the best men are ours: for 'tis ill hap
> If they hold when their ladies bid 'em clap.

Epilogue to King Henry VIII

'TIS TEN TO ONE

There are ten kings in Europe, I am the one queen. (Note— When Mary Stuart, Queen of Scots, was forced to abdicate in favor of her infant son in 1567, Elizabeth became the only ruling queen and remained the only one until her death. As for the kings: (1) Rudolph II was Emperor of Austria, Germany, and Bohemia from 1576 until 1612; (2) Ivan IV, The Terrible, was Tsar of Russia from 1533 until 1584, and Theodore from 1584 to 1598; (3) James VI was King of Scotland from 1567 to 1625; (4) Johan III was King of Sweden from 1568 to 1592; (5) Philip II was King of Spain from 1556 until 1598. He also ruled Portugal and The Netherlands; (6) Stephen Bathory was King of Poland from 1575 until 1586, and Sigismund III from 1587 to 1632; (7) Frederick II was King of Denmark from 1559 until 1588, and Christian IV from 1588 until 1648; (8) Henry III was King of France from 1574 to 1589; (9) Henry was King of Navarre from 1572 until 1589 when, as Henry IV, he assumed the dual title of King of Navarre and King of France (1589–1610); (10) Murad III was Sultan of Turkey from 1574 until 1595. In the Chronological Order *—"1955 Guess," Appendix B, the play *King Henry VIII*, was written in 1583.

THIS PLAY CAN NEVER PLEASE ALL THAT ARE HERE:

When I am disclosed to be Shake-speare, the announcement will displease many people

SOME COME TO TAKE THEIR EASE, AND SLEEP AN ACT OR TWO;

It may be one or two centuries before the riddle is solved.

BUT THOSE, WE FEAR, WE HAVE FRIGHTED WITH OUR TRUMPETS:

The disclosure will come as a shock to many people.

SO 'TIS CLEAR THEY'LL SAY 'TIS NAUGHT:

Many will say there is nothing in the theory.

OTHERS TO HEAR THE CITY ABUSED EXTREMELY, AND TO CRY 'THAT'S WITTY!'

If the riddle is not solved for many years, this will be a great joke on the literary men of London, especially if a foreigner resolves the riddle.

WHICH WE HAVE NOT DONE NEITHER:

I have not planned this as a joke on London. I had good reasons for using the pseudonym Shake-speare. It should be realized that the English people are too close to the English forest to spot the significance of a single tree.

THAT, I FEAR
ALL THE EXPECTED GOOD WE'RE LIKE TO HEAR
FROM THIS PLAY AT THIS TIME, IS ONLY IN
THE MERCIFUL CONSTRUCTION OF GOOD WOMEN:

It will be the womenfolk who will have patience and under-standing with such a translation.

FOR SUCH A ONE WE SHOW'D 'EM:

I revealed myself in the body of the play. I was not in the Dramatis Personae. I did not speak, but I was SHOWN to the audience.

IF THEY SMILE,
AND SAY 'TWILL DO, I KNOW, WITHIN A WHILE
ALL THE BEST MEN ARE OURS; FOR 'TIS ILL HAP,
IF THEY HOLD WHEN THEIR LADIES BID 'EM CLAP.

If the ladies approve this theory, then men will be brought to the same point of view but it will take time. Some men will never be convinced.

The riddle of the epilogue of *Henry VIII*, because of the circumstances experienced in its discovery, appears very real to me. Riddles in general are weak evidence; if you see no riddle it matters little. What does matter is the full realization of the point by point parallelism in the character of Elizabeth and the character of Shake-speare. Where two mighty rivers, whose source is the same lake of classical knowledge and understanding of mankind, flow down the same valley into the sea of myriad human experience and myriad human character delineation, we expect to see these two mighty rivers become one.

CHRONOLOGICAL ORDER OF THE PLAYS
"1930 GUESS"

1590–91	*2 Henry VI* *3 Henry VI*
1591–92	*1 Henry VI*
1592–93	*Richard III* *The Comedy of Errors*
1593–94	*Titus Andronicus* *The Taming of the Shrew*
1594–95	*Two Gentlemen of Verona* *Love's Labour's Lost* *Romeo and Juliet*
1595–96	*Richard II* *A Midsummer Night's Dream*
1596–97	*King John* *The Merchant of Venice*
1597–98	*1 Henry IV* *2 Henry IV*
1598–99	*Much Ado About Nothing* *Henry V*
1599–1600	*Julius Caesar* *As You Like It* *Twelfth Night*
1600–1601	*Hamlet* *The Merry Wives of Windsor*
1601–2	*Troilus and Cressida*
1602–3	*All's Well That Ends Well*
1603–4	. . . .

1604–5	*Measure for Measure*
	Othello
1605–6	*King Lear*
	Macbeth
1606–7	*Antony and Cleopatra*
1607–8	*Coriolanus*
	Timon of Athens
1608–9	*Pericles*
1609–10	*Cymbeline*
1610–11	*The Winter's Tale*
1611–12	*The Tempest*
1612–13	*Henry VIII*

Appendix B

CHRONOLOGICAL ORDER THE "1955 GUESS"

IMITATION OF THE GREEK

1579
and
1580—*Timon of Athens*
1580—*Pericles*
1582—*Cymbeline*
1585—*Titus Andronicus*
1586—*Troilus and Cressida*

EXPERIMENTAL AND IMMATURE COMEDY

1581—*Measure for Measure*
1582—*The Tempest*
1583—*The Taming of A (The) Shrew*
1584—*The Comedy of Errors*
1585—*Love's Labour's Lost*
1588—*The Winter's Tale*
1589—*The Two Gentlemen of Verona*
1590—*A Midsummer Night's Dream*
1594—*The Merry Wives of Windsor*

IMMATURE HISTORY

1583—*King Henry VIII*
1587—*1 King Henry VI*
1587—*2 King Henry VI*
1587—*3 King Henry VI*
1588—*King Richard III*

POETRY

1583—*Venus and Adonis*
1584—*The Rape of Lucrece*
1586—*Dark Lady Sonnets*
1587—*Lovely Boy Sonnets*
1588—*Lovely Boy Sonnets*
1589—*Lovely Boy Sonnets*

MATURE COMEDY

1590—*Much Ado About Nothing*
1592—*The Merchant of Venice*
1595—*All's Well That Ends Well*
1595—*As You Like It*
1596—*Twelfth Night*

MATURE HISTORY

1591—*King John*
1592—*King Richard II*
1593—*1 King Henry IV*
1593—*2 King Henry IV*
1594—*King Henry V*

MATURE TRAGEDY

1591—*Romeo and Juliet*
1596—*Coriolanus*
1597—*Julius Caesar*
1598—*Antony and Cleopatra*
1599—*Hamlet*
1600—*Othello*
1601—*The Tragedy of Macbeth*
1602—*King Lear*

Appendix C

In the prologue to the fifth act of *King Henry Fifth*, the chorus speaks of the Earl of Essex and his military expedition into Ireland:

> "As, by a lower but loving likelihood,
> Were now the general of our gracious empress,
> As in good time he may, from Ireland coming,
> Bringing rebellion broached on his sword,
> How many would the peaceful city quit
> To welcome him!"

Taken at face value this would establish the period of composition of *King Henry Fifth* between March and September of 1599. However, the quarto printed in 1600, the quarto of 1602, and the quarto of 1608, have no prologues and no epilogue. It was not until the printing of the First Folio in 1623 that the prologues and the epilogue were made public. Were the prologues written at the same time as the main body of *King Henry Fifth* or at a later date? Pope, Warburton, and others hold that the choruses were inserted at a later date. *Henry Fifth* dates itself but we have no way of ascertaining whether 1599 is an original date or a revision date. One authority estimates that fourteen of the thirty-seven plays underwent thorough revision by Shake-speare and that most of the remainder received partial revision. Such extensive rewriting at a date sometimes many years after the original draft of the play, might introduce allusions to current events which would give a false impression as to when the play was first composed.

Bibliography

ADAMS, JOSEPH Q. *A Life of William Shakespeare*, Boston: Houghton Mifflin, 1923.

ANDERSON, MAXWELL. *Eleven Verse Plays*, New York: Harcourt, 1939.

ANTHONY, KATHERINE. *Queen Elizabeth*, New York: Knopf, 1929.

BAKER, GEORGE P. *John Lyly*, New York: Henry Holt, 1894.

BALDWIN, T. W. *On the Literary Genetics of Shakspere's Poems and Sonnets*, University of Illinois Press, 1950.

BOAS, FREDERICK S. *Queen Elizabeth in Drama*, London: Allen, 1950.

BOSWELL-STONE, W. G. *Shakespeare's Holinshed*, London: Chatto and Windus, 1907.

BROOKE, TUCKER. *Essays on Shakespeare and Other Elizabethans*, Yale University Press, 1948.

BROOKS, ALDEN. *Will Shakspere and the Dyer's Hand*, New York: Scribners, 1943.

BROWN, IVOR. *Shakespeare*, Garden City, N.Y.: Country Life Press, 1949.

BUCK, PHILO M. *The Golden Thread*, New York, Macmillan, 1931.

CAMPBELL, LILY B. *Shakespeare's Histories*, Huntington Library, 1947.

CARROLL, SYDNEY W. *The Imperial Votaress*, London: Constable, 1947.

CHAMBERLIN, FREDERICK. *The Private Character of Queen Elizabeth*, New York: Dodd, Mead, 1922.

CHAMBERLIN, FREDERICK. *The Sayings of Queen Elizabeth*, New York: Dodd, Mead, 1923.

CHAMBERS, E. K. *William Shakespeare*, London: Clarendon, 1930.

CHARLTON, H. B. *Shakespearian Comedy*, New York: Macmillan, 1938.

CLAPHAM, JOHN. *Elizabeth of England*, University of Pennsylvania Press, 1951.

CLEMENS, SAMUEL LANGHORNE. *Is Shakespeare Dead?*, New York: Harper, 1909.

DARK, SIDNEY. *Queen Elizabeth*, New York: Doran, 1927.

DOWLING, JENNETTE, and LETTON, FRANCIS. *The Young Elizabeth*, London: Elek, 1948.

DUTHIE, GEORGE IAN. *Shakespeare*, London: Hutchinson's, 1951.

FFRENCH, YVONNE. *Six Great Englishwomen*, London: Hamish Hamilton, 1953.

FROUDE, JAMES ANTHONY. *History of England*, New York: Scribner, 1906.

GASSNER, JOHN. *A Treasury of the Theatre*, New York: Dryden, 1951.

GLOVER, ALAN. *Gloriana's Glass*, Stellar Press, 1954.

GREG, W. W. *The Shakespeare First Folio*, London: Clarendon, 1955.

HALLIDAY, F. E. *Shakespeare and His Critics*, London: Duckworth, 1949.

HARBAGE, ALFRED. *Shakespeare and the Rival Traditions*, New York: Macmillan, 1952.

HARRIS, FRANK. *The Women of Shakespeare*, New York: Mitchell Kennerley, 1912.

HARRISON, G. B. *Story of Elizabethan Drama*, London: Cambridge University Press, 1924.

HARRISON, G. B. *Shakespeare's Tragedies*, Oxford University Press, 1952.

HOLMES, NATHANIEL. *The Authorship of Shakespeare*, New York: Hurd and Houghton, 1867.

HOTSON, LESLIE. *Shakespeare's Sonnets Dated*, London: Rupert Hart-Davis, 1949.

HOTSON, LESLIE. *Queen Elizabeth's Entertainment at Micham*, Yale University Press, 1953.

HUBLER, EDWARD. *The Sense of Shakspeare's Sonnets*, Princeton University Press, 1952.

HUME, DAVIS. *History of England*, Philadelphia: Porter and Coates.

HUME, MARTIN. *Life of Sir Walter Raleigh*, New York: McClure, 1904.

HUME, MARTIN. *The Courtships of Queen Elizabeth*, New York: McClure, 1904.

INNES, ARTHUR D. *England Under the Tudors*, New York: Putnam, 1911.

JAMESON, ANNA. *Shakespeare's Heroines*, New York: Burt, 1934.

KNIGHT, G. WILSON. *The Wheel of Fire*, Oxford University Press, 1949.

LAWRENCE, W. W. *Shakespeare's Problem Comedies*, New York: Macmillan, 1931.

LEE, SIR SIDNEY. *A Life of William Shakespeare*, New York: Macmillan, 1925.

MACCALLUM, M. W. *Shakespeare's Roman Plays*, London: Macmillan, 1925.

MARTIN, SIR THEODORE. *The Works of Horace*, London: Blackwood.

MAUGHAM, W. SOMERSET. *The Summing Up*, Doubleday, 1938.

MUMBY, FRANK A. *The Girlhood of Queen Elizabeth*, Boston: Houghton, Mifflin, 1909.

MURRY, J. M. *Shakespeare*, London: Cape, 1954.

NEALE, J. E. *Queen Elizabeth*, New York: Harcourt, 1934.

NEILSON, W. A., and THORNDIKE, A. H. *The Facts About Shakespeare*, New York: Macmillan, 1913.

NICOLL, ALLARDYCE. *Shakespeare*, New York: Oxford University Press, 1952.

NORMAN, CHARLES. *The Muses Darling*, New York: Rinehart, 1946.

ORD, HUBERT. *Chaucer as the Rival Poet in Shakespeare's Sonnets*, London: Dent, 1921.

PARROTT, THOMAS MARC. *Shakespearean Comedy*, New York: Oxford University Press, 1949.

PARTRIDGE, A. C. *The Problem of Henry Eighth Reopened*, Cambridge: Bowes and Bowes, 1949.

PEMBERTON, CAROLINE. *Queen Elizabeth's Englishings*, London: Trubner, 1899.

PRESSON, ROBERT K. *Shakespeare's Troilus and Cressida*, University of Wisconsin Press, 1953.

REESE, M. M. *Shakespeare, His World and His Work*, New York: St. Martin's Press, 1953.

RIDLEY, M. R. *Shakespeare's Plays*, New York: Dutton, 1938.

ROBERTSON, J. M. *The Problems of the Shakespeare Sonnets*, London: Routedge, 1926.

ROWSE, A. L., and HARRISON, G. B. *Queen Elizabeth*, London: Allen.

SCHICK, JOHN. *The Spanish Tragedy of Thomas Kyd*, London: Dent, 1907.

SHAW, G. B. *Dramatic Opinions and Essays*, New York: Brentano's, 1906.

SHAW, G. B. *The Dark Lady of the Sonnets*, New York: Brentano's, 1910.

SKEAT, WALTER W. *Shakespeare's Plutarch*, London: Macmillan, 1875.

SPENCER, THEODORE. *Shakespeare and the Nature of Man*, New York: Macmillan, 1949.

SPURGEON, CAROLINE. *Shakesperian Imagery*, Cambridge University Press, 1935.

STEWART, CHARLES D. *Some Textual Difficulties in Shakespeare*, Yale University Press, 1914.

STRACHEY, LYTTON. *Elizabeth and Essex*, New York: Harcourt, 1928.

STRICKLAND, AGNES. *A Life of Queen Elizabeth*, New York: Dutton, 1906.

SUGDEN, EDWARD H. *A Topographical Dictionary*, London: Manchester University Press, 1925.

SYMONDS, JOHN. *Shakspere's Predecessors in the English Drama*, New York: Scribner, 1908.

TERRY, ELLEN. *Four Lectures on Shakespeare*, London: Martin Hopkinson.

TILLYARD, E. M. W. *Shakespeare's Last Plays*, London: Chatto and Windus, 1938.

TILLYARD, E. M. W. *Shakespeare's History Plays*, New York: Macmillan, 1946.

THORNDIKE, ASHLEY H. *Tragedy*, Boston: Houghton, Mifflin, 1908.

THORNDIKE, ASHLEY H. *English Comedy*, New York: Macmillan, 1929.

WALDMAN, MILTON. *England's Elizabeth*, Boston: Houghton, Mifflin, 1933.

WALDMAN, MILTON. *Elizabeth and Leicester*, Boston: Houghton, Mifflin, 1945.

WILSON, E. C. *England's Eliza*, Cambridge: Harvard University Press, 1939.

ZOCCA, LOUIS R. *Elizabethan Narrative Poetry*, Rutgers University Press, 1950.